DISABILITY, CULTURE,

Alfredo J. Artiles, Series Editor

Dismantling Disproportionality

A Culturally Responsive and Sustaining Systems Approach

María G. Hernández, David M. Lopez, and Reed Swier with Jaspreet Kaur

Foreword by Edward Fergus

TEACHERS COLLEGE PRESS

TEACHERS COLLEGE | COLUMBIA UNIVERSITY

NEW YORK AND LONDON

Published by Teachers College Press,® 1234 Amsterdam Avenue, New York, NY 10027

Copyright © 2023 by Teachers College, Columbia

Front cover photo by Reed Swier.

Library of Congress Cataloging-in-Publication Data is available at loc.gov

ISBN 978-0-8077-6736-8 (paper)
ISBN 978-0-8077-6737-5 (hardcover)
ISBN 978-0-8077-8123-4 (ebook)

Printed on acid-free paper
Manufactured in the United States of America

We dedicate this book to students, families,
communities, and educators who have made a commitment
to fighting for racial equity and justice.
You are our inspiration.

Contents

Foreword

The outcome of disproportionality reflects a complicated narrative of the United States' racial project. The core narrative of this racial project is that ideas of superiority and inferiority tied to racial classifications are rational and can be codified into our society and institutions—for instance, the codification of school practices and policies arranged based on such notions of oppression and organized to continuously substantiate or rationalize its persistence. This is a narrative codified into understandings of youth behavior as dichotomous renderings of good/bad, reasonable/unreasonable, normal/abnormal, etc.—a narrative codified into special education classifications as bound to ideas of who has ability and disability. Disproportionality is a result of such machination of this racial project.

The work on disproportionality I began in 2004 at the Center for Disproportionality involved developing a robust process for districts to endure in grappling with this complicated narrative. This work involved many great educators in school districts and an amazingly deep-thinking group of technical assistance providers such as the book authors. *Dismantling Disproportionality* reflects a poignant and expansive discussion of what it takes to persist in addressing this complicated narrative. More specifically, this book explores the ways in which school districts, in particular the moves of leadership, need to situate the meaning and significance of this complicated narrative as central to addressing disproportionality. After nearly 20 years and working with over 120 school districts across 10 states (California, Wisconsin, Texas, Illinois, New York, New Jersey, Connecticut, Delaware, Maryland, and Pennsylvania) with hundreds of educators, it is clear that the human capacity to name, unpack, and replace the history and ripple effect of this country's original sin involves multi-layered strategies and a long-term commitment. Robert Carter, one of the NAACP lawyers on the 1954 *Brown v. Board of Education* case, stated that the true significance of the case was to finally situate the need for humanity to be a centerpiece for how Black children are treated in schools. The work this book is encouraging educators to embark on involves continuing to redesign schools by placing Black experience at the center of reform strategies.

The authors embody in this book the spirit of compassion, empathy, critical thinking, and educational thought necessary in addressing disproportionality. You'll be able to experience in this book a conversation on the journey on which school districts embark once identified with patterns of disproportionality. Such a conversation allows for understanding that disproportionate patterns are not eliminated in a short few years but rather unraveled over many years of intentional and staged implementation. As you read this book, take lessons from these district examples and create your own implementation roadmap.

—Edward Fergus

Preface

As educators, we have made a lifetime commitment to addressing racialized inequities in our work, society, and lives. The work of dismantling is a way of living, not a JOB. The first and second authors have experienced personal harm and exclusion in the K–12 education system that led us to our career paths.

The first three authors are trainers and technical assistance providers in State Education Agencies (SEAs) and Local Education Agencies (LEAs) throughout the country. The first three authors have left our families for 2–3 days mostly every week to partner with districts. At times, we would drive to districts, leaving our homes at 5:00 A.M. aiming to arrive at our training site by 8:00 A.M. In each district we travel to, we find a home away from home. In our own journeys of disrupting racialized disproportionate experiences and outcomes for historically and currently marginalized children, families, and communities, we've also had disappointing and difficult days. We have left asking ourselves, "What are we doing here?" "Can we support a change here?" On such turbulent days, we lean into the love we have for children and families in districts and school spaces. We also lean into the several inspiring educators who committed themselves to the work, are brave when others are not, and persist even in turbulent waters. They are the beacons of the work, and are an inspiration.

We have learned of the power of transformational relationships in our work. Through building relationships with educators in districts and schools, we have been able to create communities of educators who authorize themselves to push other educators to lead, challenge racialized inequities, and confront the status quo of the cemented views that those with power and privilege often hold for our students, families, and communities. They authorize themselves to transform their districts and schools and be an agent of change. We also see the power of relationships when an educator in a district or school reaches out once we have left to share how our work together changed their practice, changed their beliefs of our most vulnerable children.

Our work has always centered on being honest with districts and schools about the lift of engaging truthful and difficult conversations that center on how race and racism impact students, families, and fellow educators. We have also been transparent with districts that educators cannot be culturally responsive to students, families, colleagues, and communities of differences until they engage in the journey of personal critical self-reflection. We have been clear that disproportionality is not a child issue, it is an adult issue, and it's not about fixing children, it's about fixing a racist system. When we are not brave, bold, and truthful about who is excluded and harmed in school spaces, we fail students, families, and communities. When harm is happening to students, and no action is taken, we are culpable.

Writing this book has been a labor of love and hope. Our hope is that as you read this book, you are able to use it as a guide on how to tackle your community's disproportionality; that you are able to lean into the work as a messy journey, and not a linear "fix it" moment, and you realize that once you are on the path, that it is possible. The promises and challenges we lay out may mirror what you see occurring in your district and school, and we want to encourage you to stay on the path. We want you to walk away with the realness of what it means "when the rubber meets the road." This is the work!

Acknowledgments

We are extremely grateful to leaders and educators who trusted us over multiple years to partner alongside them as they grappled to tackle their disproportionality head on. We learned with them and we learned through them. For the many students and families that we met, we have been forever transformed through your sharings and bravery.

We are thankful to the mentors and scholars who have come before us and built the foundation for CfD's work. We want to thank Dr. Eddie Fergus who has been a mentor and a visionary leader in developing solutions to address disproportionality. The first author learned so much from Dr. Fergus while in the field with them. The second author learned so much from them as a mentor and graduate school advisor. Their mentorship left an everlasting imprint on how to authentically engage the work. We are thankful to Dr. Pedro Noguera for always reminding us to lean into adaptive work, while employing the technical support. We want to thank Dr. David E. Kirkland for pushing us to assess the effectiveness of the CfD model. We are extremely grateful to Dr. LaRuth Gray. Dr. Gray's mentorship, advice, and wisdom was invaluable and timely. We continue to be inspired by the many scholars who we build our work from and who continue to challenge the status quo: Dr. Gloria Ladson-Billings, Dr. Geneva Gay, Dr. Beth Harry, Dr. Russell Skiba, Dan Losen, Dr. Aydin Bal, Dr. Anne Gregory, Dr. Django Paris, Dr. Wendy Cavendish, Dr. Margaret Beale-Spencer, and Dr. Beverly Tatum.

We started writing this book at the start of the COVID-19 pandemic and like many experienced various life setbacks and challenges. We are extremely grateful to Dr. Alfredo Artiles for mentorship, encouragement, guidance, patience, and grace. We continue be in "awe" of Dr. Artiles' scholarship and authenticity. We are very appreciative to Brian Ellerbeck for the ongoing guidance, patience, and encouragement. We are grateful for all our friends, educators, and colleagues who have reviewed our work to make this book better.

We are grateful to our CfD Advisory Board who spent many hours consulting with us, offered mentorship, and were always present at our CfD annual conference. Their guidance was priceless and advanced our work.

We want to thank the state where CfD resides for re-imagining how disproportionality for students with an IEP by race/ethnicity could be tackled. The work of CfD would not have been possible without their support.

We want to thank the many associates and directors of CfD who also made a commitment to doing the work. In particular, we are grateful to Dr. Patrick Jean-Pierre for his vision for how to do the work ethically, responsibly, and authentically. We want to thank Dr. Hui-Ling Sunshine-Malone for her powerful work with our youth around disproportionality. We learned so much from all of the young people who poured in countless hours of work as part of the youth wing of CfD. We want to thank our youth for all they taught us. We are also grateful to Jaspreet Kaur for bringing together multiple years of CfD data, and using her skills as a data analyst to enhance the case studies with data. Jaspreet's contribution as a senior research associate to the book is recognized as a "with."

Finally, we want to thank our families for their ongoing support for allowing us to leave our homes weekly to follow our life passion and for still holding space for us to share our experiences in the field. Thank you for your grace and empathetic listening.

Dismantling Disproportionality

CHAPTER 1

Introduction

We may have to defend a radical approach to democracy that seriously
undermines the privilege of those who have skillfully carved that privilege
into the foundation of the nation. We will have to adopt the position of
consistently swimming against the current.

(Ladson-Billings, 1998, p. 22)

Springfield High School[1] sits on top of a hill, looming over the medium-sized northern town inhabited by a mix of big city runaways and racially diverse working-class families. A little less than half of the students in the high school are students of color, predominantly Black and Latinx,[2] and a bit more than half of the total student body is considered "economically disadvantaged" (The State[3]). In many ways, this school functions as the epicenter for public schooling in Springfield because it operates as the sole high school, where the roughly 2,000 students are all funneled.

About 15 years ago, members of the Ku Klux Klan and affiliated white supremacist groups held a rally on the very same hill on which the high school sits. They emphatically called for public demonstrations because of alleged attacks on white students, specifically from Black students in the high school. On the day of the protest, records indicate that the white supremacists were met with an even larger number of antiracist counterprotesters. This moment in the town's history embodies not only the undercurrent of racial tension that exists in the community, but also how the school itself operates as a pivotal site of conflict. Our public schools have always operated as a microcosm, or mirror even, of our larger society. Springfield offers an example of how schooling is much more than four walls and a chalkboard, but rather, a platform to reinforce systemic racism that continues to churn out disproportionate experiences and outcomes for the most marginalized students and families in our society.

In 2018, the Center for Disproportionality (CfD) was a training and technical assistance provider for the Springfield School District, following the District's state citation under the Individuals with Disabilities Education Act (IDEA) for over-suspending Black and Latinx students with an Individualized Education Plan (IEP). On one particular day in late fall of that year, four of the CfD associates (trainers) were tasked with engaging all high school staff in a full-day session highlighting some of the key understandings related to Culturally Responsive Education (CRE). For this session, our content ranged from *"What are the key components of Culturally Responsive Education?"* to *"What does it mean to have white privilege?"* Each of us had about 30 participants in our respective rooms, including classroom teachers, administrators, resource staff, and paraprofessionals. As was our practice, we cued up our PowerPoints, stuck up our chart papers, and dove into the work of building the capacity of the participants in front of us to develop the knowledge, skills, and abilities to become culturally responsive educators.

As we stepped out of our session for our scheduled lunch break, it was clear from each of our faces that we all had experienced some form of intense pushback in our rooms. One CfD associate was cursed at and heckled by a group of educators in the back of the room. One Black woman participant (one of just a few in the entire staff) left one of the rooms crying, overwhelmed with emotion from her colleagues' refusal to even engage in a dialogue about the causes of disproportionality.

Disproportionality runs rampant in schools where feelings of isolation, resistance, and hostility are pervasive responses to attempts at uncovering inequities; where anger and defensiveness take over and where there's an inability to reimagine what students truly deserve. Disproportionality is the outcome of a history of schooling in the United States that was always set up to exclude marginalized students and communities through beliefs, policies, procedures, and practices (BPPPs). These BPPPs manifest in many ways, including through exclusionary discipline and White-centered curricula; schooling that was formed by whiteness as the operating norm; and a system that all too often replicates the anti-Black racism that is a ubiquitous part of the United States. The above example of Springfield should not serve to lambast a particular school, community, or group of educators. Rather, it outlines some critical layers of how school inequities continue to exist. Through uncovering our process and the work of over 15 years of in-district training and technical assistance, this book aims to provide a much more expansive look at district-based disproportionality.

WHAT IS DISPROPORTIONALITY?

During training sessions in partnering districts, associates would start with defining disproportionality and unpacking how disproportionality is measured. This would often take place during an opening circle,[4] asking participants to share their name, roles, and their own definition of disproportionality. There were always a wide range of responses from, "disproportionality means an unequal playing field" to "disproportionality is unfair." Associates would subsequently offer participants two definitions,

Table 1.1. Disproportionality Definitions

U.S. Department of Education Definition:	YCfD Definition:
Disproportionality is . . .	Disproportionality is . . .
The over-representation of a specific group in special education programs or disciplinary outcomes relative to the presence of this group in the overall student population, and/or	The outcome of institutionalized racism and bias that result in discriminatory beliefs, policies, and practices, which negatively affect historically marginalized[5] groups in contrast to privileged groups.
The under-representation of a specific group in accessing intervention services, resources, programs, rigorous curriculum and instruction relative to the presence of this group in the overall student population.	

which you can see in Table 1.1, from the U.S. Department of Education and from the youth wing of the CfD, the Youth Technical Assistance Center on Disproportionality (YCfD) (see Table 1.1).

As they always do, the young folks who are continually impacted by disproportionality offer a much more powerful understanding of disproportionality as is evident by their definition. Building on the government's opaque definition that highlights the over- and underrepresentation of a specific group in an outcome area (in the case of CfD, special education assignment and/or suspensions), YCfD pushes us to grapple with the evil underbelly of disproportionality itself. The youth make the direct connection to root causes that lead to disproportionality: institutionalized racism; discriminatory beliefs, policies and practices; and a history of power and privilege for some and marginalization for others. To that end, CfD operated under the definition provided by YCfD in its work with districts.

WHAT IS THE CENTER FOR DISPROPORTIONALITY (CfD)?

CfD's Mission Statement:

The Center for Disproportionality (CfD) provides regional Professional Development and Technical Assistance to school districts. Our mission is to disrupt, dismantle, and eliminate disproportionality by building the capacity of educators to implement Culturally Responsive Equity-Based Systems that meet the needs of every student and family.

For 15 years, CfD operated through a state contract with the express purpose of supporting districts that were cited for disproportionately assigning students of color, often Black and Latinx students, into special education (often classifying them into particular special education categories and special education placements) and for disproportionate use of exclusionary discipline (e.g., out-of-school suspensions). During this time, CfD also provided regional support to regions consisting of multiple districts cited for disproportionality. The process of receiving a district citation was amplified by the re-enactment of IDEA 2004. IDEA sought to require states to actively address their disproportionality. That said, while being cited for disproportionality offered a potential entry point to engage the inequities in a school district, the citation system often fell flat in terms of holding districts accountable to sustained, systemic change. It was often the case that school districts were cited year after year without ever committing to ongoing training and development to particularly respond to the racialized outcomes present in the district. There often was a clear lack of accountability. Furthermore, if they did attempt to contend with the citation, many districts aimed at reaching compliance under IDEA rather than taking a systemic approach to identifying the root causes of disproportionality (Sullivan & Osher, 2019; Kramarczuk Voulgarides et al., 2017, 2021).

Sadly, Springfield is just one of countless examples where students of color are disproportionately negatively impacted by our education system. Racial disproportionality in disciplinary outcomes and special education classification and placement is endemic in the fabric of the American educational system. Disproportionality in special education parallels the very persistent history, highlighted in Springfield, of chronic socioeconomic and racial inequalities that relate to the country's history of exclusion and denial of educational opportunities to students of color, multilingual students, and students with disabilities (Losen et al., 2013). Thus, it is important to draw the distinction that disproportionality is not solely a special education issue as it is often seen; rather it is an outcome of broader educational inequality (Kramarczuk Voulgarides, 2018). That said, special education classification and suspension disproportionality data were simply the entry point for CfD to tackle the root causes of disproportionality (Fergus, 2017; Kramarczuk Voulgarides, 2018; Milner, 2020). What always festered below the surface layer data, the numbers on the page, was the true scourge of the American educational system—embedded white supremacist systems that continue to be fostered and maintained by BPPPs. CfD offered a way forward that was grounded in culturally responsive-sustaining education (CR-SE[6]), a pedagogical approach to schooling that is built on welcoming and affirming the identities and experiences of every child.

A DEEPER LOOK AT BELIEFS, POLICIES, PROCEDURES, AND PRACTICES

Schools are a particularly harmful institution for young people. Trouble gets made because schools engender it, exclude it, and ultimately work hard to simply erase it. Schools try to make trouble invisible, most often by attempting to eliminate the young people who are working so hard to make it visible.

(Shalaby, 2016, p. 152)

Disproportionality is linked to historic forms of systemic racism and is entrenched in our educational system's BPPPs. To create systemic change, we must reframe how we look at "the problems" in education—refusing to resort to the blaming and so-called fixing of students and their communities, but rather, interrogating the system itself. To systematically address disproportionality, we must focus on mindset shifts or the beliefs held by educators. The beliefs that individual educators hold about students of color and their communities become systemic beliefs codified in policies and procedures that are enacted through their practices. Policies and procedures can also be unwritten guidelines that educators are expected to operate under. The practices then become the ways that we enact our beliefs that are either aligned or not aligned with the policies and procedures of a school/district. These beliefs are the mental models, assumptions, values, and dispositions that our educators hold, both explicitly and implicitly, about our educational system and the students, families, and communities it serves.

For example, educators and the schools/districts in which they work often hold the belief that Black students, wearing particular clothing or hairstyles, are demonstrating inappropriate behavior or a more coded justification, "not demonstrating professionalism" (Knipp & Stevenson, 2022). In other words, the devaluing of Black students' cultures is "often equated with poor academic performance" (Ladson-Billings, 2021). All of which becomes code for not conforming to cis-gendered, white normative school culture. As a result, educators and school systems will codify this belief in their policies, like the code of conduct, and disproportionate disciplinary referrals for Black children may be the result. In this way, a disproportionate outcome and school experience for Black students is grounded in a *belief*; in racist ideology held by individuals and the system itself. The belief is then codified in a uniform policy that lives in the district, etched in school manuals and maintained through the *procedures* and *practices* of excluding Black students from school—teachers and administrators send students out of class and often home, for being out-of-compliance. This is how BPPPs continue to reinforce systemic racial disproportionality.

There are several bias-based beliefs that are pervasive in our educational system that call for our shared understanding and deeper unpacking. The following list is not exhaustive, but offers framing for core beliefs that we know contribute to racial disproportionality (Fergus, 2017):

1. **Color-Evasiveness**[7] is a dominant belief that purports seeing and talking about race as problematic. Individuals that hold a color-evasive lens contend that "seeing everyone the same" is actually the fairest way to engage difference. Color-evasiveness sounds like: "I do not see color, I see behavior;" "I do not care if the student is white, Black, purple, green, or polka dot, I treat all students the same regardless of color." The impact of such a belief discredits and denies the role that racism plays in the lived experiences of various

racial groups and obscures its role in systemic inequities. In fact, we are often left with blaming the individuals and communities for the impact of systemic racism when we maintain a color-evasive lens (Bonilla-Silva, 2003).

2.   *Deficit Thinking* places the blame of achievement and opportunity gaps on students, families, and their communities. Deficit thinking sounds like: "If Black families and communities cared more about education, their children would do better." Deficit thinking, like color-evasiveness downplays or denies the role of systemic racism. In addition, deficit thinking pathologizes students, their families, and communities while simultaneously discounting the role of educational systems in manufacturing and maintaining racial inequities. Much of the foundation of deficit thinking is based on fallacious genetic deficits and the myth of a culture of poverty (Valencia, 1997).

3.   *Poverty Disciplining* focuses on punishing the behaviors and thinking held by people from low-income backgrounds. Poverty disciplining moves to change the behavior of these individuals to reflect that of the white middle class. Poverty discipline sounds like: "When students do not conform to school culture and rules, we must punish them, or they will not know how to operate in the real world." It is important to note that while this belief does not explicitly focus on race, it is often used as a proxy to blame Black and other people of color for the conditions of schooling and their academic achievement (Fergus, 2017, 2019).

REALITY CHECK: SCHOOLING CONDITIONS FOR BLACK AND LATINX STUDENTS[8]

The above beliefs are deeply rooted in our educational system and translate into policies, procedures, and practices that are disproportionately impacting Black students, in particular. For example, research has shown that preschool teachers are more likely to look for signs of challenging behavior of young Black children—especially young Black boys—in comparison to young white boys (Gilliam et al., 2016). Research has also shown that Black children receive harsher punishment for similar behaviors as their white counterparts and are often punished for more subjective behavior such as disrespect and insubordination as opposed to more objective behavior such as smoking (Skiba et al., 2002; Skiba & Williams, 2016). Additionally, the ACLU (2020), *Cops, and no Counselors* report, which analyzed the Office of Civil Rights data from 2015 to 2016, found that: Students of color are more likely to go to a school with a police officer [SROs], more likely to be referred to law enforcement, and more likely to be arrested at school. Nationally, Black students are more than twice as likely as their white classmates to be referred to law enforcement. Black students are three times as likely to be arrested as their white classmates, and in some states, Black girls are over eight times as likely to be arrested as white girls. During the 2015–16 school year, 1.6 million students attended a school with a sworn law enforcement officer and no counselor.

Although ambiguously titled, School Resource Officers (SROs) are certified law enforcement officers assigned to schools on a long-term basis. What becomes one's experience of schooling if you are more likely to be criminalized than supported? Researchers for some time now have highlighted the concept of the school-to-prison pipeline (Wald & Losen, 2003), but what becomes clear when we examine the conditions and experiences that our most marginalized communities far too often face is that schooling becomes much more of a school-to-prison nexus (Meiners, 2007), where schools themselves are sites of exclusion, violence, and isolation—chief markers of our prison system. As we layer these systemic barriers, it should become quite clear how racist ideologies and explicit and implicit biases continue to push students of color, and Black students even more acutely, out of the classroom and often problematically into special education assignment and placement.

THE ROLE OF CULTURALLY RESPONSIVE EDUCATION

CfD centered CRE as a remedy for ever-present bias-based beliefs serving as the catalyst for addressing policies, practices, and procedures contributing to the continual disproportionality across the nation. Foundational to CRE is examining the biases that educators hold so they can mitigate potential harm and more effectively affirm the ethnic and racial identities of their students through curriculum and teaching practices (Ladson-Billings, 1995a). CfD knew that we must start with the individual and ultimately connect self to the system to address disproportionality, because it is people who make policy and enact practices. CRE provided the framework for how we approached this theory of change. CfD associates often used the analogy that culturally responsive education was not an add-on to a full plate but is the plate itself and everything else should be placed on that foundation.

WHERE DO WE GO FROM HERE?

If we are serious about systemic change, based on justice and liberation for oppressed communities, it is critical that we contend with the often complicated and layered connections needed to disrupt and dismantle disproportionate outcomes and experiences. This book will provide an overview of CfD's approach alongside four case studies to highlight important lessons learned.

In Chapter 2, we will unpack CfD's multi-tiered approach to engaging with district partnerships. We will provide an in-depth overview of CfD's guiding frameworks, including a further breakdown of disproportionality. We also outline the Root Cause process and CRE trainings that were ultimately CfD's foundation—core to uncovering and responding to existing inequities in a district. We will further highlight the methodology and the distinct approach that CfD used to address disproportionality through connecting BPPPs.

Chapter 3 provides a case study of the Elmer City School District. In this chapter, we will explore a district that needed to respond to the Attorney General Office's 2013–2014 complaint and investigation of over-suspending Black students alongside a state citation for over-suspending Black students with disabilities. This chapter will underscore the processes that led to developing a strategic plan centered on culturally responsive practices and the ongoing work that the Office of Pupil Support Services has led, slowly chipping away at bias-based beliefs and existing disproportionate outcomes. Further, this chapter will underscore how Elmer used data systems that calculate disproportionality to monitor their disparate outcomes.

Chapter 4 focuses on Palisades City School District. In this chapter, we will unpack the strengths and pitfalls of the role of leadership in shifting disproportionate outcomes. This chapter will further explore the impact of only focusing training and technical assistance support on district and building leadership and the lack of internal capacity built from this approach. Lastly, the shortcomings of rigid, siloed district leadership and its impact on ultimately shifting racialized experiences and disparate outcomes that exist throughout a district will be examined.

Chapter 5 will provide a case study of Hamsburg City School District. In this case study, we will explore their initial lack of readiness to address disproportionality. That said, once readiness grew, they systematized equity through data systems, the strategic hiring of an equity leader, district-led culturally responsive trainings, and centering family engagement. The story of Hamsburg stresses the impact of developing a readiness mindset in districts in order to shift disproportionality.

Chapter 6 will provide a case study of Hayward Unified School District. We will highlight Hayward Unified School District's ongoing journey to develop competency, and ultimately capacity in culturally responsive practices through a Train the Trainer (TTT) model. In addition, this chapter will address the barriers that exist when district leadership recognizes the urgency of addressing disproportionality, but wants to expedite the process without offering sufficient time and resources to effectively implement practices. We will offer perspectives from long-time, district-based CRE co-facilitators engaging with how they defined CRE as "life's work."

We will close with a chapter acknowledging key lessons learned and critical frameworks that are informing current work. We end each case study chapter with guiding questions in an effort to make this text more of a call to action than a static memorial of work from the past. Throughout our case studies, we look to challenge the notion that the measure of evaluating success in disrupting and ultimately dismantling disproportionality solely lives in the reduction of problematic data (i.e., decrease in suspensions rate, etc.) or state/federal compliance. Instead, we will argue that because disproportionality is a result of racist systems, we must focus on changing the beliefs of educators to support equitable policies, procedures, and practices. This becomes the first step before we can expect any trainings to radically change the "numbers" of disproportionality. Without this paradigm shift, policies and new initiatives will continue to fall short. Finally, the last few years have not only reinforced, but in many ways exacerbated structural and institutional inequities in the United States—inequities with clear, direct impacts on the experiences and outcomes of our students of color in our schools across the country. We hope to build on the long legacy of community, educator, and researcher activists actively pursuing and cultivating schools as sites of liberation, as environments that foundationally celebrate Black joy and Black genius; schools as full representations of the communities they serve.

CHAPTER 2

Dismantling Disproportionality

A Systemic Process to Addressing Racialized Disproportionality in Special Education and Discipline

Every system is perfectly designed to get the results it gets.

—Attributed to Donal Berwick

INTRODUCTION

Provisions for Local Education Agencies (LEAs) to monitor race-based disproportionality were introduced as part of the Individuals with Disabilities Education Act (IDEA) in 1997 within the Disabilities Education Amendment Act. In the 2004 re-enactment of IDEA, these provisions were strengthened by making monitoring and enforcement of racial disproportionality a priority focus (Skiba, 2013). This included requiring State Education Agencies (SEAs) to prioritize monitoring the outcomes of classification patterns, classification categories, placements of students, and suspension of students with an IEP by race/ethnicity. Even with such efforts, racialized disproportionately continues to be a chronic education inequity. One established claim is that the impact of IDEA as a policy is race-neutral (Kramarczuk Voulgarides et al., 2017). It recognizes race-based disproportionate outcomes, but the solutions, protections, and interventions built into IDEA do not specifically address race, ethnicity, and cultural differences (Kramarczuk Voulgarides et al., 2017). Such an approach creates the conditions for educators to view "disability" separate from race and a separation from racialized outcomes, even though disability classifications and suspensions are indeed also racialized outcomes. Within this structure, the racialized outcome is instead identified in the individual as having a deficit rather than being impacted by a racist system—justifying the usage of deficit ideology for students of color, Black students in particular (Annamma et al., 2016; Annamma, 2018). A race-neutral approach was

11

further exemplified in the ways that states were permitted to determine how they would monitor such outcomes, including establishing varied thresholds for notification citations (Fread Albrecht et al., 2012), and identifying policy, process, and procedures of LEAs to address their disproportionality once cited (Skiba, 2013).

In the Northeast, one state's approach was to create a technical assistance center to support districts who received citation notifications for disproportionality from the Office of Special Education (OSE). Such a center was the Center for Disproportionality (CfD). For 15 years, CfD offered training and technical assistance to support districts in tackling their disproportionality.

CfD was contracted by the State to:

1) Provide technical assistance and professional development services to up to 20 school districts across the state who were cited under the State Performance Plan (SPP) indicators. These indicators focus on rates of suspension and expulsion of racial/ethnic students of difference with disabilities (SPP 4a/4b), the disproportionate representation of racial/ethnic students of difference in special education (SPP 9), the disproportionate representation of racial/ethnic students of difference in specific special education classifications (SPP 10a), and the disproportionate representation of racial/ethnic students of difference classified with disabilities in restrictive settings (SPP10b)
2) Evaluate the progress of each of the identified school districts
3) Offer trainings and technical assistance support in regions where school districts are cited or at risk of experiencing disproportionality in order to build their capacity for using best practices, strategies, and tools to prevent and reduce disproportionality
4) Participate in regional planning sessions
5) Offer an annual conference

Another state-based qualification for CfD centered on staffing. The staff hired needed to have a master's degree or higher in education, special education, psychology, education administration, or public administration; and experience providing direct technical assistance to schools on issues related to disproportionate representation of racial and ethnic groups in special education. Program associates also had to have at least 4 to 5 years of experience working in schools and substantive knowledge on education reform, achievement disparity research, English as a New Language (ENL), disproportionality in special education, race in schools, and race and gender equity. An additional critical piece associates needed to possess was the skill to navigate the technical and adaptive work as technical assistance providers.

THE CENTER FOR DISPROPORTIONALITY'S APPROACH

Disrupting, dismantling, and eliminating disproportionality that exists in districts and schools requires not only a systems-based approach, grounded in theory and research, but also a robust training curriculum to engage and inspire the educators that hold the system in place. CfD's approach to systemic change in school districts relied on intersecting equity-driven school improvement scholarship with a deep understanding of disproportionality and culturally responsive education. These frameworks of understanding grounded CfD's two central pathways: the root cause analysis series and the culturally responsive education training series. The content and facilitation involved in both also drove the type of technical assistance and support that CfD offered outside of direct training sessions. This chapter will unpack the scope of CfD's work and serve to ground the reader to better understand the specific case studies in the subsequent chapters. Furthermore, in explaining the what and the how of the work, we hope to give light to the complexity and layered understanding that is critical to disrupting and dismantling the inequitable, disproportionate outcomes that continue to impact the most marginalized communities in our school systems. Through training and technical assistance (TA), CfD fought—and often struggled—to continuously offer this level of complex delivery, contending with an education system built and maintained by a history of racism and exclusion.

Approaches to Training and Technical Assistance

To support ongoing effectiveness, throughout its 15 years of existence, CfD continuously adapted content, bolstered by current research and associates' experiences in the field. CfD challenged the historic approach of TA that often operates in districts with the central goal of streamlining systems, creating coherent policy and essentially making the machine that already exists run smoother (Kozleski & Artiles, 2012). In contrast, CfD's approach carried with it a foundational focus on achieving equity while building on assets already embedded in the school community. Moreover, it was based on what education researchers Kozleski and Artiles (2012) call *transformative mediating structures*. Their methodology for TA, specifically, sits in a focus of ongoing inquiry that inevitably leads to systemic change. Kozleski and Artiles (2012) make the argument that the tools used to better understand and analyze the problems persistent in schooling must provide "opportunities to make connections between technical, situated and critical factors that undergird[ed] disproportionality" (p. 415). This work is about building the internal capacity of a district through a deeper understanding of disproportionality and equity-based systems. To that end, the facilitation of such should be grounded in processes that are co-created and inquiry-based.

In every session, whether it was during the root cause analysis, CRE training, or targeted TA support, CfD associates looked to take an iterative approach to the overall learning environment. The approach intentionally pushed participants to engage in the lift of the work; step in with their whole selves, all of their experience and expertise; and most critically, center how race, culture, identity, power, and privilege impact the academic and behavioral outcomes and overall experiences of students in their schools. Content delivery and overall collaboration was buoyed by adult learning theory (Aguilar, 2016; Knowles, 2015; Speck, 1996), which provides a basis for engaging with stakeholders as learners throughout the training and TA process. Training activities included a variety of instructional strategies (e.g., content presentation, group discussion, role play, case studies, problem-solving groups, and other participatory activities) that enhanced adult learning. CfD fully embraced the belief that adults learn together and through activities that are situated within their communities—activities that provoke reflection and critical dialogue (Aguilar, 2016; Lave & Wenger, 1991). This work was a continual balancing act—balancing how to most effectively impact the dualities that maintain systems of disproportionality and racialized disparities in our society. CfD's approach simultaneously addressed the technical and the adaptive; the heart and the mind; the individual and the system.

Frameworks That Grounded CfD's Work With School Districts

There is ample research highlighting systems change work and the ways in which institutions need to think about long-term, sustainable change (Bryk et al., 2010; Fullan & Quinn, 2016). That said, CfD engaged this scholarship through a culturally responsive foundation. Systems won't change for our most marginalized students and families[1] without a reckoning with the longstanding inequities that exist in our schools (Gorski, 2019). The foundation itself is cracked and a band-aid approach only maintains underlying systems of oppression. For example, we reiterate here that racial disproportionality in special education is an outcome of the impacts of systemic racism in general education (Skiba et al., 2008). Public schooling in the United States was built and continues to be maintained by white normative values, and beliefs, which inevitably create spaces for inequity and marginalization for anyone who does not comply with this standard. CfD built the foundation of the work through culturally responsive educational systems that engage all levels of schooling—from the teacher and student, to school and district leaders, to family and community members, to the district, state, and federal policies. The coherence and alignment in cultural responsiveness amongst these spheres of influence make systemic change possible (Klingner et al., 2005).

School and district leadership was a critical lever for change. The ways in which CfD engaged district leadership was supported by the federal and state oversight and the disproportionality citation process; the state effectively put CfD in rooms with district leaders through a district being cited. That said, CfD's theory of change relied on leadership as a catalyst of change (Bryk et al., 2010), making a district leader's participation in the TA and training process critical. Without the buy-in of superintendents, district, and building leaders, shifts for more equitable schooling fall flat and/or remain siloed in individual schools and classrooms. Furthermore, these leaders (namely principals, superintendents, and also district administrators) cultivate a growing cadre of other leaders (teachers, parents, and community members) who can help expand the reach of the work and share overall responsibility for improvement (Fullan & Quinn, 2016). Engaging leadership as a starting point for CfD framed the first of five essential supports for effective systems change.

The five *Essential Supports for School Improvement*, as outlined by Bryk et al. (2010), undergirded much of how CfD understood and implemented school and systems change. These five essential supports are: (1) *Leadership as a Catalyst for Change*, (2) *Parent and Community Ties*, (3) *Professional Capacity*, (4) *Student-Centered Learning Climate*, and (5) *Instruction Guidance*. Grounding the work in equity and culturally responsive education, CfD interpreted the essential supports in the following way (see a more detailed description in Appendix A):

1. *Recognizing School Leadership* as a change agent for equity
2. *Aligning Family and Community Engagement* plans with the historical, social, and educational needs of families and communities within schools
3. Building *Staff Capacity* in culturally responsive education
4. *Establishing Student-centered learning climate* mechanisms for social and emotional learning growth and welcoming and affirming environments
5. *Adapting Instructional guidance* systems to become relevant and asset-based to meet the needs of all students, particularly historically marginalized students

CfD intersected Bryk's work with scholarship on disproportionality, particularly as it related to the disproportionate impact experienced by students of color through special education assignment and exclusionary discipline (Skiba et al., 2016). In all training and TA spaces, it was critical for participants to have a grounding in disproportionality and culturally responsive education and how these approaches serve to uncover the realities of present-day school outcomes and experiences.

CfD'S ENTRY POINT: WHAT EXACTLY IS DISPROPORTIONALITY AND HOW IS IT MEASURED?

Because CfD's entry point was focused on addressing the state citation (see Table 2.1 for citation thresholds), the variations in disproportionality citations became critical information. In accordance with federal guidelines, a school district received a citation notification for the following set of indicators highlighting disproportionate special education and discipline outcomes:

- *Indicator 9*: Refers to disproportionate identification of racial and ethnic groups for special education and related services as a result of inappropriate identification.
- *Indicator 10*: Refers to disproportionate representation of students with disabilities by classification in specific disability categories (10a) and by placement (10b) by race/ethnicity.

Thresholds for citation notification did not change annually for indicators 9 and 10. The threshold for indicator 9 was a relative risk ratio of 2.5, for 10a, 4.0, and for 10b, 2.0 (the ratios are further discussed below).

- *Indicator 4a*: Defined as a significant discrepancy in the *rate* of suspensions and expulsions of students with disabilities for greater than 10 days in a school year.

Table 2.1. Citation Thresholds by Year for 4a/4b and Significant Disproportionality

Year	2012–2013	2013–2014	2014–2015	2015–2016	2016–2017	2017–2018	2018–2019
Citation Criteria Indicator 4a: Number of school-going children with disabilities suspended over 10 days	2.70%	2.70%	2.70%	2.70%	2.70%	2.70%	2.70%
Citation Criteria Indicator 4b: Number of school-going children with disabilities suspended over 10 days by race	3.49%	3.21%	3.07%	2.98%	3.03%	3.03%	3.08%
Significant Disproportionality	2.0	2.0	2.0	2.0	2.0	2.0	2.0

- *Indicator 4b*: Known as significant discrepancy in the *rates* of out-of-school suspensions and expulsions of greater than 10 days in a school year of students with disabilities by **race and ethnicity**.
- *Significant Disproportionality*: Characterized by the incidence, duration, and type of disciplinary actions, including suspensions and expulsions by race/ethnicity set through a relative risk ratio.

These citations flagged a district's need to fix an ongoing problem with disproportionality. It is important to note that the large majority of districts that CfD partnered with over the years predominately had citations for Black, Latinx, and multi-racial students and rarely white and Native/Indigenous students. There were limited citations for Native/Indigenous students because of their low population size and isn't indicative of the level of marginalization that Native/Indigenous students experience in schools. In partnering with a cited district, CfD looked to further unpack the ways in which disproportionality manifested across the district's school population. To do so, CfD utilized three prominent methods to calculate disproportionality: Composition Index, Risk Index, and Relative Risk Ratio. Below, we define these methods with examples.

Methods to Calculating Disproportionality

Composition Index calculates the proportion of students by race/ethnicity in a particular outcome. Composition indexes are used to determine if a particular group is over or underrepresented in a particular outcome. For example, Latinx students make up 25% of a school population, but receive 50% of all suspensions in a given year. This would signify that Latinx students are overrepresented in suspensions.

Risk Index/Rate is the representation of a racial/ethnic group in a particular outcome in comparison to the total enrollment of that specific racial/ethnic group. For example, 30 Black students are involved in the disciplinary outcome out of a total 100 Black students enrolled. The Risk Index or Rate for Black students stands at 30%. In other words, Black students are at a 30% risk of being represented in a disciplinary action.

Relative Risk Ratio, also referred to as "relative risk," is the risk of one racial/ethnic group in comparison to the risk of all other racial/ethnic groups to experience an outcome. A risk ratio of 1 indicates a racial/ethnic group has equal risk in comparison to all other groups for a particular outcome; less than 1 means underrepresentation of a racial/ethnic group; and higher than 1 means a racial/ethnic group is at an elevated risk in comparison to the other racial/ethnic groups. For example, if 50 out of 100 Black students were suspended, creating a risk of 50%, whereas only 50 out of 200 students from all other racial/ethnic groups were suspended creating a risk of 25%, the relative risk ratio for Black students is 2, which means Black students are 2 times more likely to be suspended as compared to all other students. The relative risk ratio is often a preferred method of calculation because it offers a comparative index of risk (Klingner et al., 2005).

TRAINING AND TECHNICAL ASSISTANCE SUPPORT MODEL

Regional Training and Technical Assistance

One central piece to addressing disproportionality across the state became the regional trainings offered through CfD. In the late spring/early summer, CfD would meet with the regional support partners to: (1) identify the regional training that would be offered in the school year based on the need in the region, (2) discuss which districts had received a citation notification or were at-risk to receive a notification across the region; and (3) to determine if CfD would prospectively start partnering in the district through regional trainings or as a CfD embedded district. That is, would the work move from the region and into specific districts needing support?

CfD built a multi-tiered approach to regional trainings with three potential pathways of support: (1) cited districts or those at-risk for citation only attended 4 full-day regional trainings, (2) cited districts or those at-risk for citation attended 4 full-day regional trainings with 2–3 days of technical assistance support, and (3) intensive training and TA support where 2–3 districts would be targeted in the region to conduct a root cause analysis and condensed CRE training. Decisions to determine which district(s) would engage in which training was a joint conversation with partners in the region. Such a decision was also dependent on the district's readiness.

The content of the 4 full-day trainings offered through the region ranged from foundational culturally responsive training to culturally responsive and alternatives to suspensions, to cultural variation and behavior pathways. Regardless of the training focus, session 1 would start with establishing session norms and norming disproportionality, and the causes of disproportionality. Districts who made progress through the 4 full-day training sessions were approached to receive the additional 2–3 days of technical assistance support.

District Training and Technical Assistance

An overview of the four phases of CfD work with districts is discussed in this section. CfD implemented a multiphase approach to district partnerships (see Figure 2.1). It is important to note that CfD work, including the phases, training modules, and technical assistance approach resemble

Figure 2.1. Multiphase Professional and Technical Assistance Plan

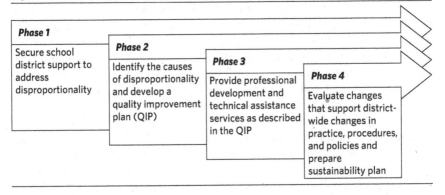

the latter 5 years of CfD's existence. These modifications were made based on the lessons learned in the first 10 years of CfD operating within the state. The first phase of any partnership started with securing the school district's support to addressing the disproportionality that exists in their community. Again, this process was initiated by the district receiving a state-level citation for racial disproportionality in special education and/or discipline outcomes for students with an IEP. That said, CfD's focus in Phase 1 was primarily about relationship building—engaging the leadership as a critical leverage point and carrying out a series of meetings with district leaders to develop a foundation for potential work and an honest conversation about how their district would be addressing racial inequities. In the initial meeting with prospective partnering districts, CfD would highlight that the district had a racialized outcome and race-based conversations would be centered. Further, the director and associate(s) would engage the leadership to anecdotally gauge if they were ready to authentically have race-based conversations. CfD associates knew that systemic change relied on the district leaders' understanding and ability to move the work. These initial meetings also allowed associates to assess the readiness in the district and within the individuals leading the district. For example, if a district superintendent was not able to articulate the importance of doing equity work and looking at their disproportionality head on, it was clear that readiness to engage this work would be an ongoing issue. This tension around barriers to systemic change based on readiness will be unpacked further in our case study chapters (see Chapter 5 specifically).

Phase 2 with a district partner involved identifying the root causes for the disproportionality that was prevalent in the specific district. The disproportionality outcome data was the entry point to uncovering the systems that exist that enable such outcomes to persist. In identifying root causes, CfD associates began to weave in language and understandings of culturally responsive education. For example, we observed that when schools and classrooms were not welcoming and affirming to every child, particularly marginalized students, they continued to see the same outcomes highlighting disproportionate impacts to these same students and communities. The message conveyed to partnering districts was that the only way forward is developing equity-based, culturally responsive systems throughout the school community. To do so, Phase 2 offered scaffolding to implement a districtwide ongoing Quality Improvement Plan (QIP) and eventually, through the root cause analysis series, a 5-year Multi Service plan, outlining the key action steps a district needs to take to foundationally address their existing root causes to disproportionality. The root cause series itself was foundational to Phase 2 because it became the process by which root causes were identified. CfD had to submit a QIP to the state for every partnering district with concrete goals, implementation strategies, and outcomes. The QIP was co-developed with the district. Ultimately, the multi-year action plan and the QIP was required by the state to indicate how training/TA would address the district's particular citation.

Phase 3 became the critical engagement of professional development/training and TA. Districts took part in the Culturally Responsive Education Training series (outlined later in the chapter). These trainings were accompanied by TA particularly for district leadership (superintendents and leaders in central office) to successfully message and support ongoing buy-in to the work that was being undertaken in the district. Through periodic TA, associates also supported the ongoing examination and development of district-wide policies, pushing districts to make cultural responsiveness and equity the plate, the foundation to any initiative or policy that was created or reviewed. Districts were driven to compare the current beliefs and practices that existed in their schools to more culturally responsive revisions and approaches offered by CfD and leaders who were a part of this new inquiry-based group.

The final phase of CfD work, Phase 4, was focused on the evaluation of systemic change in the district—specifically, evaluating the beliefs, policies, procedures, and practices (BPPPs) that have led to or impeded achieving more equitable outcomes and experiences. Associates walked district leaders through the QIP process, measuring the progress made based on the initial goals developed. They also solidified a long-term, 5-year plan to push for internal accountability and capacity building in the district itself. The overarching goal by Phase 4 was always about capacity building—that is gradually releasing a district to take on all short-term and long-term equity efforts independently.

Root Cause Analysis Training

CfD supported districts to co-identify the *root causes* of disproportionality in their district and schools. This first included the lead contact in the district organizing a root cause team, including individuals who served at different

levels—district leadership, school building leaders, teachers, pupil personnel staff, paraprofessionals, parents/caregivers, and community members.
CfD emphasized the importance of assembling a team that represented a
diverse range of roles and identities. The Root Cause series entailed training
sessions hosted by CfD with the school district's root cause team. These sessions aimed to develop participants' competency around disproportionality
and equity. Through this training, the district would identify the root causes
of their disproportionality and create a 3–5-year plan to create and foster
culturally responsive systems to eliminate the disparate outcomes that existed in their district community. The five-session (6 hours per session) series
is described below.

Overview of the Root Cause Analysis Training Series.[2] The goal of the
root cause analysis was to: (1) identify the possible root causes and
compounding factors of disproportionality; (2) examine and identify
BPPPs that contribute to disparate outcomes; (3) explore how race, culture, power, and privilege perpetuate disproportionality; and (4) develop
a plan designed to address identified causes. The following session descriptions highlight how CfD approached meeting these goals.

Session 1: Understanding disproportionality. The first session
of the root cause analysis process centered on developing a common
understanding of disproportionality and how it related to a district's
data. This sesssion also focused on how CfD planned to work to
build the capacity of both the individual participants and the district,
to effectively address the disproportionate outcomes and experiences
happening in the district. Participants would often hear CfD associates
say things like "this work centers race" followed by evidence and
research that highlighted the impact of race and racism on schooling.
One root cause slide from Session 1 reads, "Almost every indicator
of well-being shows troubling disparities/disproportionalities by race.
Disparities are often created and maintained inadvertently through
policies and practices that contain barriers to opportunity."[3] This
"heart and mind work" starting off in Session 1 was made possible by
a very deliberate scaffolding of group norms around "active listening"
and "speaking your truth" alongside an unpacking of the core tensions
(Pollock et al., 2010) that inevitably arise when educators are working
to achieve racial equity. Additionally, during this session, partnering
districts would receive their citation data book. The book simplified the
Office of Special Education's notification to offer an interpretation of the
citation.
Session 2: Examining disproportionality. Effectively analyzing
disproportionality was a foundational aspect of the root cause
process. Session 2 focused on building participants' capacity to do

this through unpacking data workbooks compiled for the district- and school-level teams. The district-level data book provided practitioners with the opportunity to explore district-level data to more deeply understand disciplinary patterns across the district as a whole. The root cause team collectively reviewed school district data, coupled with policies, procedures, and practices to identify and map the causes of disproportionality. CfD collected student-level discipline outcome data disaggregated by race/ethnicity, gender, grade, and IEP status. The analysis carried out included: the district enrollment, count of behavioral incidents, count of students involved in the behavioral incidents, count of referrals, IEP classifications/de-classification, and suspensions. For each of these, associates trained participants to use the composition index, risk ratio, and the relative risk ratio to see where disproportionality existed. This data analysis was used to further understand which student communities were most disproportionately impacted in general education, by special education assignment, and within the discipline system (through behavioral referrals and suspensions). For example, the data book incorporated social identity intersectionality (e.g., race, gender, and IEP status), data that frequently highlighted how Black boys and particularly Black boys with disabilities are disproportionately referred for discipline and suspended in a given district.

The school-level data book provided educators the opportunity to explore school-level data and to understand disciplinary patterns in their respective school buildings. As participants analyzed disproportionality through the three methods of calculation included in the workbooks, they started to see critical patterns that became points of interrogation and also, at times, moments of fragility and defensiveness. Participants often exemplified this with comments like "this data can't be right!" or "well, there are so few students of color so it must skew the numbers." Participants would also often start recalculating the data. CfD pushed groups to see the patterns and uncover the research-backed realities—like how white students are referred for discipline more frequently for objective reasons (e.g., smoking, vandalism), while Black students are referred for discipline for more subjective reasons (e.g., loitering, excessive noise) (Skiba et al., 2002). This became a key point of the training to highlight the need for culturally responsive education. That is, if educators are not understanding the ways in which we carry bias and operate within a structure imbued with racism and marginalization, school-based outcomes and experiences will continue to show the unequal treatment of marginalized communities.

Session 3: Getting to root cause. In Session 3, participants continued to develop a basic hypothesis around the data patterns they unpacked in the prior session. CfD associates continued to push participants to more deeply assess their district- and school-based discipline system, including the code of conduct, behavioral referral forms, behavior and academic interventions and supports, and school discipline procedures. Participants at times struggled to identify how policies and practices were impacting special education classifications and/or suspensions. These questions were placed in the context of examining the risk and protective factors that exist for students at the educational systems level, as well as how power and privilege and levels of vulnerability impact particular student groups (Spencer et al., 2006). Participants were asked to consider the following questions: What BPPPs currently embedded in the district lead to vulnerability for particular student communities? What systems provide protection? How does a deeper understanding of power and privilege help us discover and respond to systems and practices that disproportionately benefit white, affluent student communities?

Staff survey. Prior to Session 3, district leaders were asked to distribute the Staff Belief Survey. The online survey was aimed to be taken by all staff members in the district to assess staff beliefs and school-based culturally responsive practices. The survey asked respondents about their curriculum, school climate, self-efficacy, teacher-student relationships, instructional support, and responsiveness to the needs of students of color. Survey participants also completed the Perspectives on Race and Culture scale (developed by the Equity Project). This scale asked questions on color-evasiveness, deficit thinking, racial and cultural awareness, professional responsibility, and ensuring student success. The survey also included specific sections for school leaders and specific sections for instructional and noninstructional staff. It further served as a critical instrument in helping inform the district about beliefs that are directly tied to disproportionality (see Appendix B for survey example questions). Furthermore, the survey provided room for participants to add comments or thoughts. During this session, a survey analysis report was shared with participants to examine the patterns and to identify next steps.

School visits. Another critical part to CfD's work was conducting school visits. Often, if a district was small–medium size, CfD would visit all of the schools in the district; when it was a large district, CfD would visit a sample of the schools. The purpose of the visits was to assess cultural responsiveness in schools and classrooms, including school and classroom culture and climate, and looking specifically at culturally responsive practices. Schools were told that the visits were not evaluative and were used in the root cause analysis process. Associates would meet with the building leadership team to hear from them about their school. A CfD school visit tool was used to ask questions about the schools' strengths, growth areas, academic, and behavior support systems, and talk about current discipline and suspension data. The leader was asked to develop a classroom visit schedule prior to the visit. The school leader would accompany the assigned associate during the school walkthrough, and classroom visits. CfD often visited 5 classrooms using a classroom visit tool to assess if culturally responsive practices were present across various indicators (e.g., students' culture is incorporated into instructional materials in classrooms [texts, materials]). The associate would debrief with the building leaders to share noticings. School visit findings were often shared in Session 3. The school visits offered insight on how school spaces were creating the conditions for disproportionality.

Session 4: Root cause report and action planning. Session 4 focused on the root cause team identifying their root causes of disproportionality (see Appendix C for example belief, policy, and practice root cause table). At this point the district root cause team would also receive a draft of their root cause report to review. The report reflected the work that the team had engaged with in prior sessions and was used to guide next steps. Session 4 also included identifying key areas of improvement; focus areas that would form the framework of a multi-year service plan. Participants were guided by the five *Essential Supports for School Improvement* (Bryk et al., 2010) (listed earlier in the chapter) and asked to develop action steps that would directly respond to the root causes for disproportionality that existed in the district. Throughout the prior three sessions, participants unpacked district data and connected the outcomes to BPPPs that currently existed. In identifying successful action steps, they now had to think about what systems or practices needed to shift that would help disrupt and dismantle disproportionality. For example, often in the Essential Support of *Family and Community Engagement*, districts were pushed to create a plan to be more responsive to the voices and experiences of families of color and those with lower socioeconomic status (SES) in the district. Providing voice to those that have been excluded becomes foundational to shifting experiences and behavioral and academic outcomes in a school system.

Session 5: Root cause: Multi-year action planning. As Session 4 supported how districts dug into the root causes for disproportionality and connected them to BPPPs living in districts and schools, Session 5 became critical to putting thought to paper. CfD recognized that making connections and developing new understandings and skills is one thing, but systems do not shift without strategic planning that becomes codified and actionable. Session 5 was very much about rolling up the sleeves and getting all of the pieces on paper. Participants were divided into five teams based on their expertise to develop the plan. They were guided to develop a plan that would target their disproportionality, while leveraging their existing initiatives that would lead to impacting their disparate outcomes (e.g., restorative practices, curriculum revisions). They wrote out incremental goals for the upcoming years. The strategic plan process also involved discussing how the long-term work would be messaged throughout the district and community and how the current root cause participants would continue supporting the plan's long-term implementation, alongside additional key stakeholders depending on each focus area. While the strategic plan was started during the session, team members would often independently come back together to finalize the plan draft. The CfD associate would offer the district feedback on the draft plan. At times, CfD found significant variation in action planning skills as well as a desire to have exemplars from other districts that have been successful in addressing disproportionality. During this timeframe, districts would also receive their final root cause report. The report included: (1) citation notification, district- and school-level discipline, and suspensions data; (2) field notes from the trainings; (3) staff survey and school visit findings; (4) a synthesis of the policy and practice analysis conducted during the sessions; (5) the belief, policy, and practice root causes; and (6) CfD recommendations based on the identified root causes.

During the Root Cause process, CfD often recognized that districts needed a deeper grounding in culturally responsive education. In balancing the adaptive and technical aspects of the five Root Cause sessions, it was often the case that participants struggled with their own defensiveness, fragility, and biases in a way that impeded the analysis process. It becomes difficult to move a group through the analysis of disparate outcomes and tie them to foundational root causes that are steeped in systems of (delusions of) white supremacy, power, and privilege, if individuals have not done their own self work. Even while interlacing the Root Cause Analysis training series with CRE frameworks and the modeling of culturally responsive facilitation, the need for further training was often evident.

Associates also completed field notes after each training to identify the progress participants were making throughout the sessions. This offered the associate insight on individual and group growth, and worked to identify where the associate had to push the root cause team further. A synthesis of the field notes was included at the start of the root cause report to offer a context to non-participants on what occurred during the sessions.

GROUNDING THE WORK IN CULTURALLY RESPONSIVE-SUSTAINING EDUCATION

What Is Culturally Responsive (and Sustaining) Education?

Culturally Responsive pedagogues, led by the seminal work of Gloria Ladson-Billings (1994) and Geneva Gay (2000), center race, culture, and the critical importance of challenging the BPPPs that have white supremacist roots—roots that continue to negatively impact students of color as well as intersecting marginalized identities. Culturally responsive education seeks to create classrooms and school culture that welcome and celebrate the social identities of every child by taking a critical look at the systems and historic structures that have reinforced inequity in our country and by extension, our schools. CRE calls for both a historical reckoning and an active look at the racialized realities of our school systems, which highlights the core of the work and the essence of what Ladson-Billings referred to as a "pedagogy of opposition."

In her work, *But That's Just Good Teaching,* Ladson-Billings (1995a) offers the three necessary criteria of culturally relevant teaching: "(a) Students must experience academic success; (b) students must develop and/or maintain cultural competence; and (c) students must develop a critical consciousness through which they challenge the status quo of the current social order" (p. 160). In *The Dreamkeepers (1994)*, Ladson-Billings leads us to synthesize eight principles of culturally relevant pedagogy:

1. Communication of High Expectations
2. Active Teaching Methods
3. Practitioner as Facilitator
4. Inclusion of Culturally and Linguistically Diverse Students
5. Cultural Sensitivity
6. Reshaping the Curriculum or Delivery of Services
7. Student-Controlled Discourse
8. Small Group Instruction

Twenty years after *But That's Just Good Teaching*, the word "sustaining" became adjoined to our understanding and application of culturally responsive education (Paris, 2012). In doing so, we are asked to think about how culturally *sustaining* pedagogies support students' ability to maintain their personal, cultural, and linguistic competencies while also gaining access to dominant cultural competence (Paris, 2012). For example, often students of color and linguistically diverse students bring with them understandings that are different from the white normative culture pervasive in schools in the United States. Students of color, excluded from the perceived value of whiteness that is lauded in schools (Ladson-Billings & Tate, 1995) through BPPPs, are often seen through a deficit lens—having needs and problems rather than assets worth sharing. In what has become an anchor text in the responsive education world, in 2019, New York State released the CR-SE framework. They define CR-SE as "[education that is] grounded in a cultural view of learning and human development in which multiple expressions of diversity (e.g., race, social class, gender, language, sexual orientation, nationality, religion, ability) are recognized as assets for teaching and learning." The NYSED CR-SE framework further offers four principles critical in developing a CR-S environment: (1) Welcoming and Affirming Environment, (2) High Expectations and Rigorous Instruction, (3) Inclusive Curriculum and Assessment, and (4) Ongoing Professional Learning (NYSED, 2019).

Using the principles originally developed by Ladson-Billings and Gay, CfD focused the work around CRE by first and foremost, centering race. Taking a race-conscious lens to address what was often "the elephant in the room" became the entry point to authentically building critical competence with educators. Highlighting that race-based bias and racism have led to disproportionate negative outcomes for students of color in schools was integral in being "responsive" to the current realities within our schools.

CfD centered race in order to understand individual and systemic racism, while also engaging an intersectional lens examining the layers of marginalization that come with varying social identities (Crenshaw, 1991). To do so, it was critical to build a CRE foundation by starting with critical social identity self-reflection. We can't be culturally responsive if we do not understand self, our personal identities, and the impact they have on our students, colleagues, and community members. The work of examining self, of our own cultures, histories, and personal narratives, builds the muscle and practice to be open to this same dialogue and process with students and families. This continuous self-reflective work became the thread that ran through six distinct culturally responsive education focus areas: (1) Culture, (2) Race/Identity, (3) Power/Privilege, (4) Vulnerability, (5) Stereotype Threat, and (6) Microaggressions. The overarching goal in utilizing these particular focus areas was to develop a race conscious mindset amongst each core group of practitioners. Without such a mindset, educators were unable to understand why they were not culturally responsive and sustaining to students of color much less make the necessary systemic, practice, and policy changes in schools.

CfD Culturally Responsive Education Training

I had a lightbulb moment today during our session. We were asked if there was a time when we realized we were _____. For me, that blank was the word, white. It hit me today that I cannot pinpoint a time or an age that I realized I am white. But, I have known since elementary school that I am not black. For most of my life, I haven't thought about being white at all. This training has helped me to see that I need to take a deep look at what being white means in order to better be able to communicate with, to advocate for, and to teach students of color.

—CRE Training Participant

The training relates to my daily interactions with students, colleagues, and parents. This training has infiltrated every part of my being—I'm not exaggerating.

—CRE Training Participant

The participants' comments highlight a couple critical aspects of CfD's CRE Training Series. First and foremost, the five-session training series looks to engage a full paradigm shift of not only how educators see and experience schooling but also how they engage with their lives outside of the school building. The primary goal of the CRE series was to push participants to develop a more critical, questioning lens—a lens that connected a history of BPPPs to present-day experiences and outcomes.

Overview of the CRE Training Series

Session 1: Principles of culturally responsive education: What is culture and what relevance does it play in schools aiming for equity? The first session aimed to support practitioners in developing a common language; an understanding of CRE, but even more foundationally, terms like: equality, opportunity, access, equity, fairness, race, ethnicity, class, and culture. Through an unpacking of terms, session 1 highlighted disproportionality as a systemic problem that requires personal urgency. The training centralized the importance of developing ongoing critical self-reflection, examining how identity, power, and privilege impact school-based outcomes. Session 1 began the process of recognizing institutional and organizational structures in schools that perpetuate inequities.

Session 2: What do we need to know about ourselves relative to race and power in order to better understand our students and their families in ways that enhance teaching and learning? Session 2 explored how participants have come to understand what race and racism means and grow their ability to effectively engage in "race conversations." Through an exploration of social identities, participants drew connections between power, privilege, and systemic school inequities. In this session, participants were pushed to move past an "equality lens" where everyone gets the same thing and everyone is seen as equal, and into an equity mindset where we develop systems based on student and family need, while being color-conscious and acknowledging the impact of racism in schools and overall society.

Session 3: How Does Racial and/or Ethnic Identity Impact Racially and Ethnically Diverse Students? Session 3 focused on participants sharing their "earliest race and culture-related" memory. The session examined how racial identity development is also happening for students and the ways schools play a role in supporting or impeding the development of a healthy identity. The process is supported by developing an understanding of various racial and ethnic identity development models (Cross, 1995; Helms, 1995). The aim of this session was for educators to increase their level of awareness around how their social identity positions them in terms of their power and privilege. The session also called participants to make connections to the broader socioeconomic and political context. In moving through the activities and content, they continued to think about "culturally appropriate" strategies and ways to build caring classroom communities.

Session 4 and Session 5: What Policies and Practices Will be Changed, Given Our New Perspective? The last two sessions pushed to position educators in a place to affect change—to take content and their growing ability to understand self and others and work to shift school policies and practices to be more equity driven and culturally responsive. Session 4 continued to challenge how individuals engage the everyday actions of cultural responsiveness, starting with breaking down the concept of microaggressions. Participants learned the difference between microassaults, microinsults, and microinvalidations, which offered a critical framing to use in everyday interactions. This session also unpacked stereotype threat (Steele, 2011) and the impact of having singular stories for students. Furthermore, the *dual axis model of vulnerability* became key to planning for policy and practice changes in schools. This model aims to have educators identify where spaces of risk and spaces of protection occur for marginalized students in the educational system. For example, what student groups experience high risk and low protection as a result of school BPPPs? Knowing this, what protective factors (systems that protect further marginalization, e.g., a school breakfast program that everyone has access to) need to be created and for whom? (Beale Spencer, 2006; Spencer et al., 2006).

Session 5 was then spent on walking through CfD's CRE Toolkit to build participant's capacity to use each tool with their own school community. The CRE Toolkit included: (1) a CRE classroom and school visit/observation tool to assess culturally responsive classrooms and schools, (2) a culturally responsive problem-solving team protocol (i.e., Guardians of Equity) aiming to address BPPPs, (3) a curriculum audit tool to assess curriculum for cultural responsiveness, and (4) an Early Warning Systems Equity calendar aiming to support districts and schools in an ongoing data inquiry process to address disproportionality. Finally, the last session would end with participants sharing what personal commitment they were making to CRE.

CRE Data Collection: CoBRAS and Field Notes

CfD was cognizant of the need to assess the impact of the CRE training sessions. CfD used the *Color-Blind Racial Attitudes Scale* (CoBRAS) (Neville et al., 2000) to assess shifts participants were making as a result of undergoing the CRE training. This scale measures "unawareness of racial privileges, unawareness of institutional discrimination, and unawareness to blatant racial issues." Results from the scale developers (Neville et al., 2000) suggest that higher scores on each of the CoBRAS factors and the total score are related to greater: (1) global belief in a just world, (2) sociopolitical dimensions of a belief in a just world, (3) racial and gender intolerance, and (4) racial prejudice. This survey was carried out between CRE sessions 1, 3, and 5.

Associates also completed field notes after each training to identify the progress participants were making throughout the sessions. This offered the associate insight on individual and group growth, and identified where CRE teams needed to be pushed further.

THE TECHNICAL ASSISTANCE PROCESS

Equity and disproportionality work in education, work that looks to shift systems, becomes much more than a set of trainings. In the case of CfD, a robust, systems-based approach to equity relied heavily on technical assistance. CfD married the Root Cause and CRE Training Series application with intensive and ongoing technical assistance. At base, this was relationship and capacity building and directly supporting individuals to do the work. Successful technical assistance not only built internal capacity within the district, but fostered a level of sustainability for district personnel to continue to push CRE and equity-based work. Such work, particularly occurring after the Root Cause and CRE trainings, often included the Guardians of Equity protocol, and CRE co-facilitation and coaching support.

Guardians of Equity: Culturally Responsive Equity-Based Problem-Solving Protocol

One key lever to grow district capacity within the technical assistance process was through the modeling and training of the Guardians of Equity protocol (GoE protocol). To effectively address disproportionate and disparate outcomes in a district, it is integral that there is a continual process of examination and analysis of data. Similar to a Plan, Do, Study, Act (PDSA) process, the GoE protocol leverages district and school teams' ability to gather disaggregated data and come together to unpack not only what the data is saying, but also to establish a plan of action moving forward. The plan focused on BPPPs connected to specific disproportionate data points that the districts and schools would address. The GoE protocol sought to center students, not as problems to be fixed, but instead, developing solutions focusing on BPPPs that would lead to more equitable outcomes. To that end, the GoE protocol becomes a culturally responsive problem-solving approach that ensures that there are equitable outcomes for every student. The protocol was aimed to be used across any problem-solving team.

There are seven phases of the GoE protocol. The intention is for district and school teams to walk through each phase throughout the year, with the same frequency of a typical progress monitoring cycle (every 6–8 weeks). Each phase (listed below) has a process and a list of questions that become critical to focusing on equity and culturally responsive education principles.

Guardians of Equity Phases

Phase 1: Reflecting on the current state of affairs in the district and/or school. Phase 1 focuses on equity and culturally responsiveness, asking those engaged in a GoE protocol to think about where equity and CRE are present and where they are not present in the school/district. Phase 1 also focuses on the "for whom"—is there equity for students? Staff? Families and community members? A move to Phase 2 is possible with a clear understanding of equity strengths and weaknesses in the school/district. It also examines what is already working well in the district in an effort to build on top of existing effective practices.

Phase 2: Disaggregating data. Phase 2 requires individuals to uncover key trends/patterns in their data. An example of this is when districts analyze their behavioral data and determine what student groups are most disproportionately impacted by exclusionary discipline (e.g., referrals and suspensions).

Phase 3: Identifying root causes. In Phase 3, the protocol connects the data points that were identified above to root causes for disproportionality. This process occurs through identifying the BPPPs that connect to the data points highlighted and answering questions like "How do BPPPs contribute to inequitable outcomes?

Phase 4: Identifying solutions. Phase 4 is about connecting the data and the BPPPs to potential action-oriented solutions and grounding them in equity and cultural responsiveness.

Phase 5: Establishing a progress monitoring timeline. To move through phase 5, the protocol asks users to establish a timeline for how and when the proposed solutions will occur. It is critical here to also identify who will be on the team that will be monitoring the action steps.

Phase 6: Examining fidelity. Phase 6 asks guiding questions to ensure that there is a plan to know if the proposed solution(s) is working or not, which requires potential training of stakeholders and an understanding of what the data will look like if the implementation is successful.

Phase 7: Reflecting on desired state of affairs. Phase 7 becomes an open forum to reflect on the past phases of implementation and to think of new ideas and best practices to take into a new progress monitoring cycle. What seemed to have a positive impact that the team may want to look into further? What practices should be replicated at a systems level? What may we still not know that we want to find out?

CfD associates often modeled the GoE process with partnering districts and then offered ongoing technical assistance to ensure fidelity in implementation. The GoE protocol and support in carrying it out always offered a telling look at the district's true commitment to antiracist equity work. That is, districts would consistently need to be pushed to center race, to ensure data was disaggregated and to not gloss over the critical questions that helped to uncover the inequities within the district. This push was emblematic of much of CfD's technical assistance—encouraging educators to name the elephants in the room; imploring leaders to create the space for difficult dialogues; asking the questions that are rarely asked. Outside of the GoE process, this level of support was particularly offered in districts that had moved into a cofacilitation and ongoing coaching process.

CO-FACILITATION AND COACHING

CfD's theory of change was grounded in the belief that it was critical to build internal capacity in a district. That is, for districts to have the skills to lead the work independent of CfD. Key to this effort was the coaching and co-facilitation process. After a district was trained through the CRE series, they were always encouraged to identify individuals that were able to dive deeper and build their own capacity as in-district trainers. Through a gradual release process, in-district educators, alongside CfD associates, would train additional cohorts in CRE. Depending on comfort and prior experience, co-facilitators would take on sections of the content while CfD took a backseat (and scrupulous notes). Associates and co-facilitators would meet prior to the training sessions to unpack content. That said, during the training, if key questions or content highlights were missed by the co-facilitator, the CfD associate would step in to support, but focused on a shared delivery and not on flexing expertise or highlighting a co-facilitator's miss. Each co-facilitated training was followed by a posttraining debrief. The posttraining debriefs often opened with "How do you think it went?" which was then followed by a level of healthy and necessary venting and then constructive feedback from the CfD associate. Associates often mixed in role playing when needed, trying to make each content piece in the module as clear as possible. For example, the team may spend time talking through the potential pushback that comes with discussing topics like white fragility or white privilege, having co-facilitators practice what their responses would be if and when participants resisted the new learning or said something problematic. What does it sound like to hold participants accountable? What does healthy pushback look like? The coaching work that was a part of every session became critical to motivating the ongoing work for each co-facilitator; critical to helping their technical facilitation skills meet what their heart already knew and in doing so, plant the seed for in-district growth. Coaching also extended past the delivery of training sessions and often included coaching district leaders through effectively engaging various CRE skills and tools as highlighted previously in this chapter (e.g., the GoE protocol and CRE classroom and school observation tool).

CfD aimed to engage a five-part coaching protocol where associates operated as fidelity coaches, ensuring the proper dissemination of content and facilitation in order to ultimately best support co-facilitator growth. CfD utilized the following guidelines provided by King-Sears et al. (2018) to grow the capacity of in-district employees taking on the responsibility of turn-keying the work: (1) model the intervention, (2) share the intervention's fidelity protocol—what steps will need to be followed to ensure the intervention is effectively implemented?, (3) coach the practitioner prior to implementation, (4) observe for fidelity during implementation, and (5) reflect with the practitioner using fidelity data—what did we notice and gather from the implementation that allows us to gauge effectiveness? Chapter 6 takes a deeper look at one particular district partnership that engaged in a multi-year support cofacilitation process.

THE YOUTH CENTER FOR DISPROPORTIONALITY (YCfD)

For the majority of the 15-year state grant period, CfD operated in various districts throughout the state, building relationships with educators, but missing the voice of the youth experiencing the disproportionality. CfD recognized this as a critical growth area in the late stages of the 15-year contract. Youth voice inevitably became one of the most powerful influences to CfD's last few years of work.

During the 2016–2017 school year, a doctoral candidate at the time leveraged her work with CfD and her expertise in youth-driven equity work to form the YCfD. The original group represented 15 different schools located throughout the city where CfD was located and was supported in partnership with youth advocates from the city's department of education. Grounded in Youth Participatory Action Research (YPAR), the group set out to dismantle systems of disproportionality through examining the structural inequities highlighted within their own education experiences (Malone et al., 2020). For 3 years, YCfD met biweekly. CfD associates regularly joined and supported meetings, analyzing data alongside the youth and, more than anything, learning from their expertise and experiences.

The doctoral candidate cultivated a youth-led, welcoming and affirming, critical learning space. Out of these meetings, youth interrogated and analyzed individual, institutional, and structural forces, creating and fostering disproportionality and marginalization for students, particularly Black and Latinx students. From a research perspective, they engaged in in-depth, school-based surveying and data gathering, ultimately creating policy recommendations and detailed action plans for schools to address disproportionality head on. They also presented this research to stakeholders, both at CfD's Annual Symposium and during the city's annual youth-run conference, partnering with other young people involved in restorative justice work.

YCfD forced educators to not hide, but rather to fully examine the reality of the system we are engaged with and, in many ways, the system we have created and maintained. Their voices moved student bodies, critically shifted policies at select high schools, and most certainly, fueled the work that CfD associates did in the field, in and outside of the state.

CONCLUSION

Uncovering and analyzing disproportionality in school systems was active, ongoing work. Imploring individuals to step outside what they know and how they have operated for so long does indeed feel like continually swimming against the current. Along with uncovering the ugly truths of disparate outcomes and rampant inequities, CfD did offer a pathway forward—CR-SE was and continues to be the approach school systems must take to not only shift the numbers, but to foundationally create more welcoming and affirming environments for every student. CfD knew that holistically doing this work, through self and systems, through root causes analysis and CRE training, and through TA that built internal capacity, was the only way that real transformation could occur. Through the subsequent case studies, we look to offer solutions, continued struggles, and more guiding questions that we hope will ultimately fuel the continued work we all have ahead of us.

CHAPTER 3

The Path to a Strategic Plan in Culturally Responsive Practices

Not Linear, Messy

> First the line of progress is never straight. For a period of movement may follow a straight line and then it encounters obstacles and the path bends. It is like curving around a mountain when you are approaching a city. Often it feels as though you were moving backwards, and you lose sight of your goal: but, in fact you are moving ahead, and soon will see the city again closer by.
>
> —Martin Luther King Jr.

INTRODUCTION

The first author entered Elmer City School District in 2014–2015 at the start of the first of three root cause trainings. The district committed to begin to address their disproportionality after they had been investigated by the state attorney general for their disciplinary practices that either led to in-school suspensions (ISSs) or out-of-school suspensions (OSSs) for Black children. The attorney general also highlighted in their report that Elmer's suspension rate was one of the highest rates in the nation. Elmer had also been cited by the Office of Special Education in 2012–2013 for the over-suspension of Black, Latinx, and white children with an IEP, and at-risk of a notification for Native/Indigenous and multi-racial students with an IEP (see Table 3.1 for citation notification). Table 3.1 highlights citation notifications for 4a/4b for multiple years and significant disproportionality for 2012–2013. See Chapter 2 where we describe indicators 4a and 4b in detail as well as the thresholds for citation notifications.

This chapter underscores the work implemented over 5 years to address the disparate experiences and ultimately the outcomes of students with an IEP, and students and families of color. Further, the practices that remained imprinted from CfD's partnership with the district will be discussed, including data systems, data decision-making processes, and a strategic action plan centering CRE practices. This chapter will also grapple with the lift of

Table 3.1. Elmer Citation Data Patterns 2012–2013 to 2018–2019: Significant Discrepancy and Disproportionality

	Indicator 4a (Significant Discrepancy)	Indicator 4b (Significant Discrepancy)	Significant Disproportionality
Notification Year	Suspension Rate	Suspension Rate	Relative Risk (OSS >10)
2012–2013	All SWDs–5.50%	Black SWDs–6.79%	Black SWDs–2.55
		White SWDs–3.64%	
		Latinx SWDs–5.35%	
2013–2014	All SWDs–4.70%	Black SWDs–6.13%	Not Cited
		White SWDs–2.89% (At-Risk)	
		Latinx SWDs–3.85%	
2014–2015	All SWDs–4.40%	Black SWDs–5.65%	Not Cited
		White SWDs–2.88% (At-Risk)	
		Latinx SWDs–3.66%	
2015–2016	All SWDs–2.50% (At-Risk)	Black SWDs–3.17%	Not Cited
		White SWDs–1.53% (At-Risk)	
		Latinx SWDs–2.32% (At-Risk)	
2016–2017	Not Cited	Not Cited	Not Cited
2017–2018	Not Cited	Not Cited	Not Cited
2018–2019*	Not Cited	Not Cited	Not Cited

*limited access to state citation data

SWDs = students with disabilities

large districts tackling disproportionality, and the importance of critically self-reflecting as an organization to stay on course.

WHO IS ELMER CSD?

Elmer is a relatively large school district with 42 school sites. They have close to 4,700 staff; many of the staff in the district do not live around the district, instead in the surrounding suburbs. An educator in the district highlights this best:

> There are a lot of teachers that don't live in the communities that they teach in, and it's important to live among and interact with the community that you impact.

Figure 3.1. State Test Grade 3 ELA Proficiency by Race and IEP

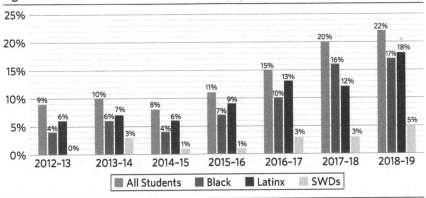

For 2012–2013, the 0 for SWDs indicates no proficiency shift.

Elmer is stamped by years of educational opportunity gaps and over-disciplining of Black children, and Black and Latinx children with an IEP. Despite Black children making up a majority of the district enrollment, they experience exclusionary discipline and higher academic disparities (see Figures 3.1–3.4). Based on 2014–2015 data (first year of CfD involvement), 50% of students in Elmer were Black. Over the years that CfD was involved with Elmer, their student demographics remained relatively consistent.

Over the 5 years of partnering with the district, the systemic beliefs, policies, procedures, and practices (BPPPs) maintained the status quo and inherent racial inequities. For instance, the district maintained a school choice

Figure 3.2. State Test Grade 8 ELA Proficiency by Race and IEP

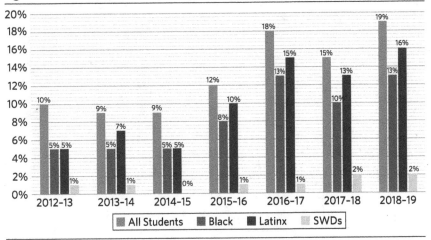

For 2014–2015, the 0 for SWDs indicates no proficiency shift.

Figure 3.3. State Test Grade 3 Math Proficiency by Race and IEP

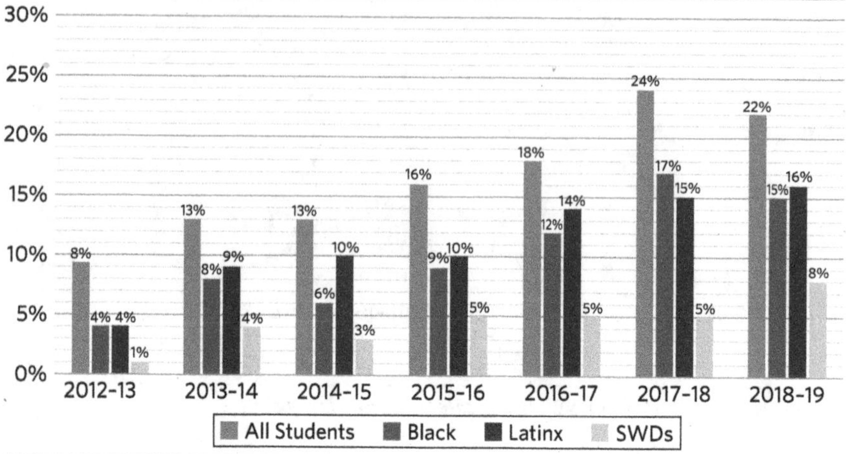

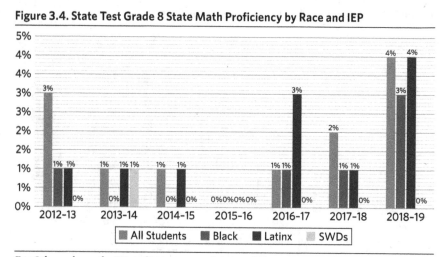

program for families to apply to schools that were not in their immediate community. Even with the choice program in place, Black and Latinx students remained in school spaces with less resources and educators with less years of experience (Milner, 2013). Yet, white students who made up 22% of the district attended schools with greater resources and educators with numerous years of experience. While rezoning would be one solution to the disproportionate experiences that Black children have in the district, there had been no efforts by the mostly white board members to rezone (Murphy, 2022; Siegel-Hawley et al., 2016).

Figure 3.4. State Test Grade 8 State Math Proficiency by Race and IEP

For 8th-grade math, 0% indicates no proficiency shifts.

Initiative overload was a noticeable factor that sometimes impeded Elmer's movement. When it seemed like there was movement, the initiative or action that was leading to progress was replaced by other initiatives. This view is highlighted by an educator in the district:

> The district as a whole has to buy in from the lunch staff all the way up to the superintendent has to buy into a program or reasonable set of programs that actually work to support students that are having difficulty. Right now our district is using a shotgun approach to using a scattered amount of programs with little follow through or continuity.

Elmer also lacked systemic accountability and critical organizational self-reflection on how initiatives can lead to interrupting the harm of Black students and overall disproportionate outcomes. While there were district wide initiatives (e.g., restorative practices, school choice, leadership development, diversity recruitment, personalized learning, K–2 literacy focus, among others) that had the potential to lead to change, schools operated as decentralized systems within the district. That is, based on observations and participation in multiple district and school leadership meetings, the CfD associate noticed that the district allows schools to operate independently and focus on school-level goals with limited oversight on how school goals should be connected to the overarching district goals (e.g., addressing disproportionate discipline referrals and suspensions, academic disparities, and initiatives).

CONTEXTUALIZING CHRONIC DISPROPORTIONALITY IN ELMER

Elmer has struggled with high suspensions for many years. Several outside agencies, including the attorney general, have investigated disciplinary practices in the Elmer school district. According to the attorney general report, issued in 2013 and based on 2011–2012 discipline data, there were two available consequences for students if referred for disciplinary action. These were ISSs and OSSs. According to the report, 35% of all students in *all grades* received at least one teacher referral; in the *middle grades* over 50% of students received at least one teacher referral; 1 in 5 students received at least one ISS; 1 in 3 at the middle school; and nearly 20% of students in the district received an OSS at least once and more than 33% at the middle school level. The attorney general report also highlighted racial disparities in disciplinary referrals and actions. For example, 1 in 10 Black students in grades 6–12 were recommended for Superintendents Hearings while conversely 1 in 20 white students were recommended. It is important to note that Superintendents Hearings often result in students being suspended out of school for several days and missing classroom instruction. Black students were routinely disciplined for "Other Disruptive Incidents," which often resulted in an OSS. Additionally, in the 2011–2012 school year, Black students were twice as likely as white students to receive a teacher referral, an ISS, or an OSS for "Other Disruptive Incidents."

Additionally, an outside consultant found that despite the high number of suspensions in the district, there were a large group of community members and staff who thought the district should be more punitive. The consultant also found 1 in 7 elementary students and 4 in 10 middle school students received an OSS in the 2011–2012 school year. Additionally, the consultant highlighted 23,555 days of instruction were lost due to OSSs.

When CfD started working with the district in the 2014–2015 school year, their overall district disciplinary referral count was 30,451 and there were 12,563 suspensions. Elementary schools totaled 5,004 referrals and 1,573 suspensions, K–8 and middle schools had 20,505 referrals and 8,876 suspensions, and the high school had 4,942 referrals and 2,414 suspensions. From 2014–2015 to 2018–2019 the disciplinary referral drop for elementary schools was 38%, K–8/middle schools was 47%, and high school was 31% (see Figure 3.5). Similarly, elementary school suspensions declined 48%, 35% at K–8/middle schools, and 17% at the high school (see Figure 3.6). While disciplinary referrals and suspensions declined, disciplinary referrals and suspensions remained higher for Black students, relative to other racial/ethnic groups. Achievement data for Elmer school district indicated there were racial disparities in both 3rd-grade math and ELA (see Figures 3.1 to 3.4). White and Asian students outperformed Black and Latinx students. In the 8th grade, the disparities persisted.

Figure 3.5. Changes in Referrals by School Level

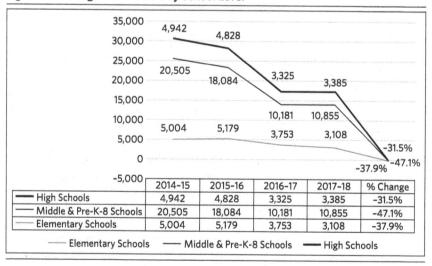

	2014-15	2015-16	2016-17	2017-18	% Change
High Schools	4,942	4,828	3,325	3,385	-31.5%
Middle & Pre-K-8 Schools	20,505	18,084	10,181	10,855	-47.1%
Elementary Schools	5,004	5,179	3,753	3,108	-37.9%

——— Elementary Schools   ——— Middle & Pre-K-8 Schools   ——— High Schools

Figure 3.6. Changes in Suspension by School Level

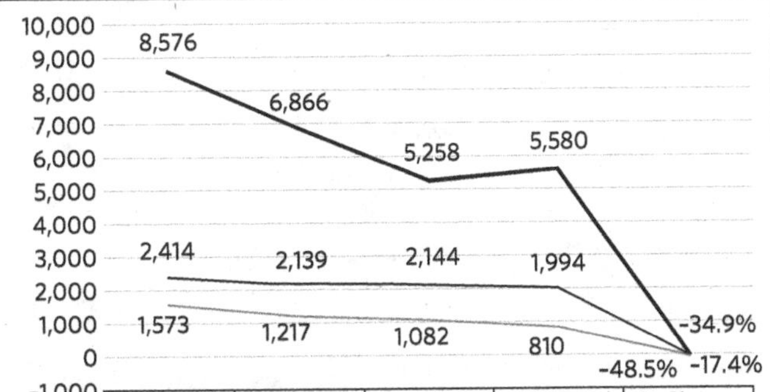

	2014-15	2015-16	2016-17	2017-18	% Change
High Schools	2,414	2,139	2,144	1,994	-17.4%
Middle & Pre-K-8 Schools	8,576	6,866	5,258	5,580	-34.9%
Elementary Schools	1,573	1,217	1,082	810	-48.5%

High Schools ——— Middle & Pre-K-8 Schools ——— Elementary Schools

BIAS-BASED BELIEFS AND DISPROPORTIONATE OUTCOMES

As framed in Chapter 1 and discussed in Chapter 4, one explanation for high disciplinary and suspension data patterns and academic outcomes at Elmer lives with the persistence of bias-based beliefs (Harry & Klingner, 2014). Staff in Elmer completed the staff surveys (see Chapter 2 for greater description) in 2014–2015, 2016–2017, and 2018–2019. The findings demonstrated minimal shifts in the overall scale of Perspectives of Race and Culture. While respondents consistently scored high on ensuring student success, and relatively high on holding professional responsibility for the students they teach, they also scored high on being color-evasive, and low on racial awareness and knowledge (see Figure 3.7). Such results underscore that educators held a sense of professional responsibility for the students, but their success was conditioned on being color-evasive and not needing to have racial awareness and knowledge, even though the majority of students and families were of color. This sentiment is reflected by the educator's quote below:

> At my school, race is irrelevant. My approach to teaching and supporting the students is based on their needs and has nothing to do with race.

Additionally, the following qualitative responses offered by educators underscore their beliefs around color-evasiveness, punishment, and deficit thinking of students and families.

> Stop using race as an issue. Treat all kids the same and it does not matter if you are poor or rich.

Figure 3.7. Results from Perspectives of Race and Culture Survey: 2014-2015, 2016-2017, and 2018-2019

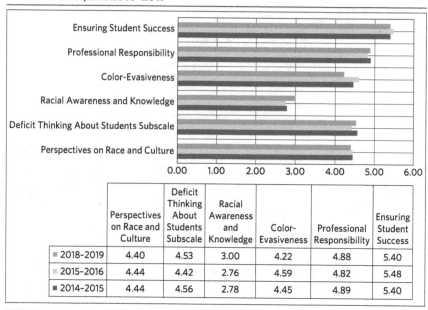

	Perspectives on Race and Culture	Deficit Thinking About Students Subscale	Racial Awareness and Knowledge	Color-Evasiveness	Professional Responsibility	Ensuring Student Success
2018-2019	4.40	4.53	3.00	4.22	4.88	5.40
2015-2016	4.44	4.42	2.76	4.59	4.82	5.48
2014-2015	4.44	4.56	2.78	4.45	4.89	5.40

I am strongly offended that anyone would look at a student's skin color and teach that child differently. I have NEVER looked at the skin color of a child nor do I ever plan to. I was not raised to treat anyone differently pending on their skin color. I am sick of race issues being the old fall out.

It's not a race issue. It's parent/family involvement issues—values and limits being at home.

We all have different backgrounds and cultures we come from. Learning has nothing to do with whether you are black, white, purple, or green. The majority of the children's families in our district have been in this country for generations. So they have been brought up with all the same expectations and have had the same opportunities. My parents came over from another country. We have our own culture and traditions, way we speak and act when we are home. But when we are out in the community or at school, we act respectful and when we are at jobs we are professional. That has nothing to do with culture or color. That has to do with being human. Stop allowing disrespect and lack of responsibility to be hidden behind color and culture.

It's time to start pointing the finger back at the students (and parents) and away from the teachers when students don't meet expectations. It's time to stop giving all our time to the lowest level students who have the worst attendance, the worst attitudes, and the worst work ethics, because we get almost no return for our efforts. If the same energy was focused on students with high ability, good attendance, good attitude and good work ethic, we would get much more "bang for our buck."

We need to stop making excuses for students of color (or any disadvantaged students) where education is NOT a priority for the student OR their family.

A student who is failing all his classes because of behavioral and non-motivational issues does not belong in a traditional classroom with other students who are trying to learn.

The questions about race and how teachers in my school view students of certain races seems to be irrelevant. I think I can speak for most educators and staff members in my building that race is the last thing we think of. There is a large population of minority groups from all over the world in my school. When someone is having an issue in the classroom or we suspect some type of behavioral issues that affects their learning, 99 times out of 100 it is either a parenting issue or an intellectual disability.

In the survey, educators also shared that there needed to be greater consequences for students:

Consequences for behavior and parent responsibility.

More consequences for repeated actions.

Discipline needs to be tougher so students are able to understand the rules and consequences of their actions and make better choices.

Students need to be held responsible for their actions. If it is disrupting class, the students should be moved immediately.

Have metal detectors.

To that end, shifting beliefs and developing CRE practices was critical in Elmer, alongside taking a multifaceted approach in training and technical assistance given the district's size.

REMEDYING DISPROPORTIONALITY: A MULTIPRONGED APPROACH

Root Cause Analysis Process

To start addressing disproportionality in Elmer, a multipronged approach was warranted. Alongside CfD, the district also had several external partners supporting them. CfD started with a root cause analysis that included teams (i.e., building leader, teacher, and social worker/psychologist) from each school level, elementary, K–8, middle, and high school. The root cause work coincided with the 2013–2014 school year Attorney General Report's Assurance of Discontinuance.[1] Part of the attorney general's agreement included revamping Elmer's student code of conduct and training staff in restorative practices. Revising the code of conduct and training a group of staff on restorative practices had started while the root cause analysis was occurring.

The root cause process revealed that staff in the district were aware of the district's disciplinary system's problem. They also shared that the district and schools were moving in the direction toward implementing positive behavioral supports and improving classroom instruction. Throughout the root cause process, the team revealed educators' sentiments of students/families not following rules and the culture of the school, blaming parents for the lack of improvement in behavior and academics, and not valuing education. At the same time, they also exemplified how the current policies promoted were derived from a white gaze that leads to a single cultural perspective that non-white students had to fit into (Harry & Klingner, 2014). The root cause team also underscored the shortcomings of existing structures and practices, including a lack of common planning time for teachers to implement social and emotional learning and restorative practices, poor fidelity implementation of behavioral intervention teams and academic programs resulting from staff shortages and master schedules not being responsive to students' need, and a lack of behavior data collection and data usage. It was clear that the team felt like they did not have the necessary support and skills to support students. Staff also expressed that support from current partnerships from a variety of external agencies was inconsistent and not supportive of school goals. With the many external partners that existed in the district, efforts to bring all partners together and develop coherence across goals and outcomes was critical. The assigned CfD associate recommended gathering all external partners to discuss how the work was connected to specific district and school priorities, goals, and outcomes. The meeting did not happen. Not creating the conditions for clarity for staff on how district and school priorities/goals are connected impedes staff buy-in and can impact a district's progress in addressing their disproportionality (Fullan & Quinn, 2016).

The next potential steps that derived from the root cause teams across the elementary, K–8, middle, and high schools included: (1) training staff in culturally responsive education; (2) restorative practices training; (3) classroom management training; (4) creating access to more effective disciplinary models and acquiring more effective intervention programs for behavior; (5) hiring mediation specialists and coaches; (6) reviewing individual and schoolwide data, putting interventions into place, and monitoring progress; (7) sharing suspension and disproportionate data with all staff; (8) training on the student code of conduct; and (9) training/strategies on how to engage parents/caregivers.

Building a Data Culture: Guardians of Equity and Targeted School Support

In the 2015–2016 school year, post the root cause analysis, the work focused on implementing the Guardians of Equity (GoE) process (see Chapter 2) that uses data to inform decision-making in schools to shift BPPPs that are leading to disparate outcomes. One of the gaps connected to disproportionality in the district was a lack of data usage overall and disaggregated data usage particularly, to inform decision-making. School-level teams that included the building principal or assistant principal attended the sessions to build school plans to address the disproportionate data outcomes. GoE occurred on a monthly basis; however, only half of the schools attended the GoE sessions consistently. For the schools who consistently attended the GoE process, they shared in sessions that they started seeing some shifts in their disciplinary referral and suspension data. Alongside the GoE work, schools were still developing structures and supports to respond to the behavioral needs by identifying alternate ways to support student behavior rather than resorting to referrals and suspensions, which included restorative practices and Positive Behavioral Interventions and Supports (PBIS) training. Immediately with support from the Office Pupil Support Services, each school was asked to create a Behavior Intervention Classroom (BIC), where students would be sent when they needed a "time out," and/or were "struggling." The goal was to have students process how they were feeling, share with an adult what was going on, and return to their classrooms. At times, when the first author visited schools, in some schools BIC resembled a space for ISSs. That is, instead of a proactive measure to meet the student's need and to avoid exclusionary discipline like suspensions, it became a holding space for those given an ISS.

Simultaneously, in the same year, eight schools were identified by the Office of Pupil Support Services to receive intensive technical assistance based on their discipline referral and suspension data patterns, including three middle schools, two high schools, and three K–8 schools. The intensive school technical assistance support was tailored to address the specific needs of the school and targeted those with higher disparities. Prior to identifying the technical assistance support, school walkthroughs and classroom visits were conducted. Based on the school visits, the following TA needs were identified to support schools: was identified to support schools: (1) leadership development and support, (2) instructional rigor, and (3) monitoring progress of students with an IEP. The assigned associate visited each building leader monthly to offer technical assistance on planning and leadership coaching, and to examine and monitor data.

Sustaining Data Usage: Leadership Data Sessions

The GoE work continued quarterly without CfD support in 2016–2017. School-level teams continued the work that started in 2015–2016 in developing capacity to disaggregate data to inform decisions and action planning. Every 6 weeks, building leaders would receive their school-level data disaggregated by race, ethnicity, gender, IEP/non-IEP status for disciplinary referrals,

Figure 3.8. Enrollment and Discipline Referral by Race

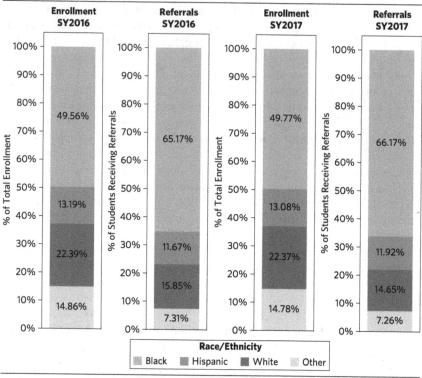

suspensions, attendance, and ELA and math benchmarks, to inform their decision-making and monitor their action plan (see Figures 3.8 and 3.9 for data examples). They came together every 6 weeks to examine their data for a half-day session. They discussed what action steps they had developed connected to their disparate data outcomes, and shared the progress they had made. Further, the district had allocated funds to hire data coaches who were assigned to schools to support school-level teams to examine disaggregated data and develop action steps. The associate also trained the coaches on the GoE protocol. That said, the assigned associate would sometimes hear from district personnel that only some of the school leaders bought into the importance of using data to inform decision-making linked to the disproportionality data.

It is important to note that in the 2016–2017 school year, the district underwent a superintendent change. The current superintendent became interim, and in 2017–2018 they were voted in as the district's superintendent. The superintendent had been a lifelong educator in the district and transitioned into their role promptly as they knew the district well through the numerous roles they had held. Their transition did not necessarily generate disruptive waves for the district as can be the case in other

Figure 3.9. Enrollment and OSS by Race

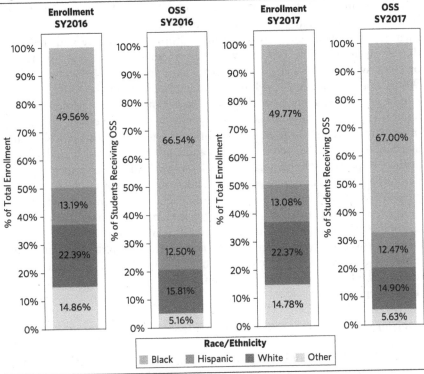

spaces. They moved forward with the agenda and initiatives that were already in place. They further invested and pushed staff to engage families that were not engaged meaningfully and who continued to be marginalized. The superintendent's push generated an office focused on family engagement. This office hired family engagement leaders to support their assigned schools, sometimes including family advocates and school–family mediators.

Efforts to Assemble the Foundation: Building a CRE Puzzle

Despite the root cause team indicating in the 2012–2013 school year that culturally responsive education training with staff was warranted, training did not begin until the 2016–2017 school year with district and school leadership. Central administration leaders, principals, and assistant principals took part in 5 full-day training sessions. The sessions validated the experiences that leaders of color had in the district. They often expressed their relief that CRE trainings had started. White participants frequently struggled in the CRE trainings, struggling to develop critical self-reflection on how race, identity, power, and privilege impact their leadership in the district and within schools with a majority of students and families of color (Khalifa, 2018). At times, white leaders, in particular principals, resisted the work by not participating and remaining silent. The assigned associate overheard them say that their school was already culturally responsive and the work did not apply to them. Often it was the principals and assistant principals of color who would share their experiences, and push the white leaders. Worth noting, conversely, white assistant principals in the CRE trainings would sometimes share how they were struggling as white leaders in their school, as they continued to actively participate, and even ended up pushing other white leaders in the training. During the final part of the CRE training, leaders received specific practices and tools they would be able to use in their respective schools (e.g., CRE classroom and school visit tools, curriculum audit tools, among others). While the assigned associate strongly pushed district leadership alongside building leaders to identify practices and tools they would consistently use, school leaders were left on their own to customize practices and tool usage based on their school. District leadership never followed up with which tool(s), nor practices, building leaders could move forward with. A few selective school leaders took it upon themselves to identify which tools and practices to move forward with and implemented them independently.

Applying CRE

In the 2017–2018 school year, the work continued with district and school leadership focused on CRE application. It was critical that leaders begin to apply CRE in their everyday practices. Additionally, CRE training started occurring with targeted teacher leaders from each building, family engagement leaders, personnel and human resources. To build the internal capacity of the district, two staff members started co-facilitating with the assigned associate. While staff who attended benefited from the work, fewer teachers were part of the staff team trained. Participants in the training shared how the CRE training had transformed them and had made them think differently about their practices. They further shared fears, including: feeling that they were not doing things that were culturally responsive; perceiving that they may be more biased than what they thought; being able to learn enough to apply CRE in the classroom; not knowing what to say; and not being able to impact change. During Session 2, a participant shared poverty as being the factor that impacts all children in the district whether they are Black, white, Latinx, Asian, or any color. Several educators nodded their head when this participant shared that. The assigned associate engaged educators by asking: How is poverty impacting students? Some participants blamed students and family, and expressed poverty disciplining statements (Fergus, 2017) (e.g., "poor kids don't know how to behave in school"). Some participants struggled with being able to see that poverty is institutional and does not sit with individuals. This offered helpful insight on the ongoing work on bias-based beliefs that needed to be tackled in the district.

In the CRE application scope of work, leaders developed their racial equity moral imperative and vision. They also identified BPPPs that were impacting Black students in their school that they would focus on shifting. Further, to practice critical self-reflection as a collective leadership team, leaders problem solved different scenarios to identify how they would address difficult incidents that had occurred in their district (see Appendix D). Through the CRE work, it was evident that leaders were sometimes seeking a silver bullet to address their racial inequities. They sometimes struggled with acknowledging that the disproportionality that occurred in the district or their school were connected to the BPPPs that they had not addressed. Similar to the CRE training, a few building principals (in particular white leaders) sometimes would not actively participate in the sessions or remained silent because they thought the work of CRE was not relevant to them or they were already enacting culturally responsive practices in their building. However, their data patterns were still disproportionate. This work underscored how district and school leadership varied in their ability to center race, culture, social identities, power, and privilege, making it clear that self-work was a critical priority in order to not perpetuate racism and racialized inequities in the districts and schools. Khalifa (2018) stresses that: "Leaders who are not critically self-aware or knowledgeable about racism, and other histories of oppression, and who do not embrace anti-oppression and social justice, will reproduce racism and other forms of systemic oppression in our schools" (p. 24). This is reflective of what was occurring in Elmer among several principals and assistant principals. The CRE work brought to light capacity building that remained to be developed in the district among leaders and a cultural shift needed to create ongoing spaces for leaders to engage in critical self-reflection (Khalifa, 2018). That is, that part of the monthly leadership development sessions warranted creating space for ongoing critical self-reflection processes.

The above sentiment was also prevalent with central administration leadership. The assigned associate worked with central administration leadership (i.e., superintendent, assistant superintendents, heads of district departments, and directors) to identify areas of racial equity improvement in the district. District leaders developed a draft plan to address their racial inequities in three areas: (1) addressing racial injustices; (2) transparency around outcomes of historically marginalized students; and (3) recruiting, hiring, developing, supporting, and retaining the most effective staff that closely mirrors the student in the district (see Appendix E for example plan draft). Throughout the yearlong sessions, the following gaps impacted the movement in the work of senior leadership: (1) no system to hold each other accountable, in particular having a designated way of following up to ensure action steps were completed; (2) no clear norms/expectations during meetings; (3) no clear objectives around weekly senior leadership meetings; (4) not having a unified vision to address the racial disproportionality occurring for Black students (e.g., some still continued to only push for "all students"); (5) lacking unification to own the disproportionate outcome of Black students; (6) missing alignment in how all initiatives in the districts were connected to student outcomes; (7) lacking space during central administration meetings for joint critical self-reflection; and (8) missing a system to monitor current initiatives for implementation fidelity, progress monitoring, and evaluation.

Through this work, it was evident that central administration leaders struggled to create a vision on how they would lead in order to tackle their race-based student disparities. Further, while district leadership expected that building leaders address their school-level disparities, they struggled with modeling it themselves. For instance, during the leadership sessions, they tended to place conversations about race, racism, and data to the side and often prioritized other agenda items. District leaders would attend these leadership work sessions unprepared and the lift often fell on the few district leaders of color whose job title and position in the district was below white district leaders (i.e., Director vis-a-vis Assistant Superintendent, or Chief Academic Officer). Even though it fell on leaders of color with lower positional power, there were efforts to start building in critical self-reflection in central administration meetings. The main challenge that the assigned associate heard from the leaders of color was that such efforts were placed at the end of the weekly agenda and often no time or limited time was left for the CRE and critical self-reflection work to occur in the meetings.

THE PROMISES OF STAYING ON THE PATH

CRE Co-facilitation

In the 2018–2019 school year a few participants who had been trained in CRE in 2017–2018 became co-facilitators with the CfD-assigned associate to build Elmer's internal trainer capacity to ultimately execute CRE trainings independently (see Chapter 6 for more detail on in-district co-facilitation). The goal was to develop a structure for school teams with individuals who had already been trained and/or were undergoing the training so that individuals who were co-facilitation could push-in to support schools to build additional training capacity. The associate assigned to the district spent 4 full days training the co-facilitators on the CRE curriculum; however, not all participated in the turn-key implementation of the training. At times, the co-facilitators did not feel ready to co-facilitate. They highlighted that they were not ready to lead or co-lead a session because some of the focus areas that are addressed in CRE were too close to them and they still had to sort out these issues for themselves (Swanson & Welton, 2018). Further, they had tensions on what to do when participants in the training were resistant to engaging in race and racism conversations, when they were unable to identify their white privileges, and when they would minimize white privilege by instead leaning on being poor or having worked hard.

Instructional coaches and new assistant principals who had not undergone the training were included. The district failed to inform CRE-selected attendees that attending the training was a requirement. At times, training attendance among participants was not consistent. Participants would often email the coordinator for the CRE training at the last minute, saying that they would not be able to attend because their principal needed them in the building. Ultimately, this led to the targeted trainees not receiving the full training. Further due to scheduling conflicts, the district canceled the fifth CRE training session.

Finally, the co-facilitation team still had to execute their primary job responsibilities; the CRE co-facilitation work was an add-on to their job. The associate partnering in the district suggested to the lead of the department that in order for internal capacity building to be developed in the districts, some responsibilities for the team members leading the training would have to be removed (see Chapters 5 and 6). CfD still ultimately left the foundation for Elmer to build CRE trainings and practices.

Data Movement

Elmer had made movements with Black students with an IEP (see Table 3.1), Black student referrals (see Table 3.2), and suspensions (see Table 3.3). That is, they were no longer cited by the State Office of Special Education from 2016–2017 to 2018–2019 for indicators 4a and 4b. There was a 41% decline in referrals

Table 3.2. Changes in Behavioral Referrals by Race

	2014–2015	2015–2016	2016–2017	2017–2018	Overall Shift*
Black	21,885	20,498	11,927	13,003	–40.6%
Latinx	–	3,453	2,154	2,238	–
White	6,931	4,893	2,649	2,186	–68.5%
Asian	455	275	147	152	–66.6%
Native/ Indigenous	382	455	182	173	–54.7%
Multi-racial	1,207	0	982	1,063	–11.9
All Students	30,860	29,574	18,041	18,815	–39.0%

*The decline total is based on subtracting the final year's referrals from the beginning year's referrals.

Table 3.3. Changes in Suspensions by Race

	2014–2015	2015–2016	2016–2017	2017–2018	Overall Shifts*
Black	8,670	7,111	5,867	5,911	–31.8%
Latinx	1,436	1,316	1,118	1,028	–28.4%
White	1,816	1,610	1,137	1,005	–44.7%
Asian	177	104	86	77	–56.5%
Native/ Indigenous	357	0	374	406	13.7%
Multi-racial	126	150	82	108	–14.3%
All Students	12,582	10,291	8,664	8,535	–32.2%

*The decline total is based on subtracting the final year's suspensions from the beginning year's referrals.

and 32% decline in suspensions for Black students between 2014–2015 and 2018–2019.

Alongside the work of monitoring district- and school-level data, and using the GoE process, the special education department had created procedures on how schools needed to respond when a behavior incident happened with students with an IEP. Such processes included first contacting the department of special education, and the building administrator, classroom special education teacher, and general education teacher who completed a checklist to assess if the incident was connected to the students' IEP. Further, data was also monitored daily to assess suspensions for students with an IEP, and monitor how many suspension days students had experienced. If students with an IEP were suspended, the special education department would contact the building administrator. Similarly, Pupil Support Services would check the daily behavior referrals and suspensions for non-IEP students and would contact school administrators when their schools exceeded the thresholds.

Building a Strategic Action Plan With CRE

In 2018–2019, Elmer recognized that centering CRE practices and family and community engagement was critical in continuing to shift their racialized disparities. The district partnered with an educational organization to support them in developing a 5-year strategic plan. Multiple stakeholders were brought together to determine the strategic plan focus for the district. The final strategic plan priorities were: (1) engage families and communities; (2) implement culturally responsive practices; (3) recruit, develop, support, and retain the most effective diverse staff; (4) personalize learning for students; and (5) provide dynamic, rigorous curriculum and instruction (see

Appendix F for specifics). While the intentions centering the above priority areas were promising, such a commitment would present its own challenges. Like many other districts and as mentioned above, Elmer is a district that consistently struggled with fully fulfilling their commitment to their priorities and initiatives, and lacked coherence. Coherence in this context is defined as a "shared depth of understanding about the purpose and nature of the work" (Fullan & Quinn, 2016, p. 1). Coherence centers the mindsets of individuals and collectively as a system holds a depth of understanding of a districts/schools' main priorities, actionable strategies, progress, and results. Internal accountability is central to coherence, which anchors the district so educators connect the purpose of the work. For Elmer as they continued on their path of reducing disparities, this meant that every stakeholder in the district needed to know about the priorities of the district, the strategies that were being implemented, and their role in implementing these priorities. It would also mean building educators' capacity to build skills, implement, and monitor the plan for implementation fidelity and impact.

Promising Shifts and Practices

The results of CfD's work in the district generated a foundation for the next steps and sustainability, including CRE, data systems, and usage of data for action. Elmer developed a robust data system that on an ongoing basis generated disproportionality data disaggregated by race/ethnicity, gender, IEP/non-IEP status, ELL/non-ELL status in attendance, behavior referrals, suspension, and academics (e.g., ELA/Math benchmarking data, MS/HS quarterly course completion, quarterly MS/HS AP and Honors enrollment) and was readily available to district and school leaders. When schools struggled with pulling data, coaches and data analysts from the Office of Accountability were readily available to support. The data analysts from the Office of Accountability would generate reports every 6 weeks for building leaders, and they had daily access to the data. In line with developing a robust data system to monitor disproportionate outcomes, the usage of data was another promising practice generated through the work. As discussed earlier, the district implemented the usage of disaggregated data to inform decision-making for 2 years through a formal 6-week cycle process. In subsequent years, they left the practice up to building leaders to execute. Some maintained the practice, while others did not, despite the Office of Accountability continuing a process of generating monthly disaggregated data reports on discipline, academics, and attendance. Shifting a district and school culture in the usage of data to inform decision-making was critical (Lachat & Smith, 2005; Park & Datnow, 2009; Roderick, 2012).

Finally, Elmer's strategic plan was promising. It laid a theory of action, goals, and implementation strategies on how the five priorities would be accomplished by 2023. These central priorities were critical to continue reducing the disparities in Elmer. They needed to be strategic on how they would allocate resources to build capacity and implement for the promises to be fulfilled. One challenge emerged early on—the plan lacked specifics on how educators would be trained on CRE practices and the allocation of the needed resources. The district thought that they could provide training on just CRE practices without educators needing to engage in the critical self-reflection work. To that end, this lack of planning resulted in no educator undergoing the 5-day training post-CfD's involvement in the district; the assigned associate was told by district personnel that the district had not allocated resources to move forward with CRE trainings. The district tried condensing the training into 2 days and only targeting a few schools using a few of the co-facilitators.

CONCLUSION: UNFULFILLED PROMISES AND CHALLENGES

There were several challenges that impeded Elmer's ability to fully fulfill their promise to implement practices that would address their disproportionality, including a lack of messaging of the work, accountability systems, not fully implementing initiatives, and the absence of a CRE training plan.

While many knew about the attorney general's involvement with the district, few knew about the CfD work that was being implemented to address their disproportionality. Like other districts who struggle with messaging, leadership as a whole did not message the work among various stakeholders in the district. For the most part, the majority who attended the CfD trainings were the only ones who knew about the work. Often, staff would arrive at trainings and they were surprised to hear that the district had disproportionate outcomes and were even unaware of the district's involvement with CfD. Additionally, there was a lack of internal and external accountability systems (Fullan & Quinn, 2016) in place that ensured progress was being made. The assigned associate observed that most initiatives while well intended were developed haphazardly without a long-term plan for long-term sustainability and impact. At times, there was limited planning offered to what the goals and sustaining strategies were for initiatives. Once the initiative they committed to was replaced with new ones, they tended to leave other initiatives behind without full implementation, rather than critically reflecting on what work would lead to shifting disproportionate outcomes for Black students and students with an IEP. Further, there were limited accountability systems in place to assess if leaders and educators were implementing with fidelity or at all. For instance, while several school-level staff had been trained in restorative practices, the practice of community circles or restorative conferences varied by school. This brings to light the particular challenges that larger districts have in fulfilling their core priorities and goals.

In addition, Elmer always had numerous outside consultants involved; however, they did not develop a plan that underscored the ways that the scope of work being implemented by various consultants would improve district level behavior, and academic outcomes for Black students and students with IEPs. During the second year of the scope of work, the assigned associate pushed the district to begin to bring together all the outside partners to discuss their work and develop a plan on how all the work was connected. This was in an effort to not duplicate services. Nonetheless, this meeting also did not happen.

Elmer had made strides in developing a robust comprehensive data system with great expertise from the analyst who was also CRE trained. This potentially had an impact on the movement they made in referral and suspension declines. Moving forward, Elmer needed to continue to use their existing district level data system that tracked data disaggregated by race/ethnicity, gender, IEP/non-IEP status, grade level, and SES in academics, behavior, and attendance to develop decision-making plans that addressed BPPPs that correlated to disproportionate outcomes. Aligned with data usage, Elmer needed to continue to set a benchmark on reducing disproportionality for every school, in particular for Black students and students with an IEP.

The following were critical next steps for Elmer as they continued to move forward: (1) creating an accountability structure; (2) sustain monthly CRE building leader/central administration work into the leadership sessions; (3) train educators in CRE and develop CRE practices; (4) align all initiatives into the new strategic plan and role of departments; and (5) create a system for monitoring for plans, programs, and initiatives for implementation fidelity, progress monitoring, and evaluation.

KEY TAKEAWAYS

While CfD's tenure in Elmer generated several lessons, the following are key takeaways learned in Elmer on addressing disproportionality. They include the following:

Addressing Disproportionality in Large Districts: Building Coherent Initiatives and Messaging

While we took on a multipronged approach to address disproportionality in Elmer, we learned that navigating large districts presents its own challenges in addressing disparities and building capacity. Elmer was drowning in initiatives and external partners, while lacking coherence in their initiatives to improve disparate outcomes (Fullan & Quinn, 2016). Throughout CfD's tenure in Elmer, there were multiple initiatives that didn't reach their full potential due to not creating the conditions for capacity building for sustainability, and the lack of messaging across the district. Messaging the work and building capacity was critical for a large district to ensure every stakeholder in the district knew about the priorities of the district, the strategies that were being implemented, and their role in implementing the district's main priorities. Messaging and building capacity among staff is critical for any district addressing disproportionality; for a large-sized district, it is even more essential. Further, for any district aiming to address disparities, they must create a structure of critical self-reflection that includes how their priorities, goals, and implementation strategies lead to shifting disproportionate experiences and outcomes for students and families. Such critical self-reflection must be grounded in CRE and equity.

Prioritizing CRE in a Strategic Action Plan

CfD supported the district by creating a pathway for centering CRE and CRE trainings. Based on the CRE focus, Elmer demonstrated their commitment to making CRE a priority in their strategic action plan. However, Elmer also had to include specifics on how educators would be trained on CRE practices and allocate resources for trainings. Their approach was to offer a 2-day training, instead of a 5 day CRE training, and did not include coaching support for staff. Coaching support is critical to continue to develop educators' skill and sustainability (see Chapter 6) (Fullan & Quinn, 2016). Further, what we learned from implementing CRE trainings in several districts was that individuals at times perceived that they did not have the skills to implement CRE in their district and schools, and still needed some coaching support (Swanson & Welton, 2018). It is critical that on-the-job coaching be embedded in the process to support educators in developing the necessary skills, tools, and the capacity to understand how to deal with their emotions, fear, confusion, and frustration when confronting the impact of whiteness when training others and supporting them directly. Elmer, like any district aiming to develop CRE as a priority, must also create a new position and/or reassign current educators to direct the CRE work, and release them from their existing job workload (see Chapters 5 and 6).

District and School Leadership Readiness

Central to addressing disproportionality in Elmer was the readiness of leaders. Elmer had monthly full-day leadership development trainings that brought district and school leaders together to build their skills and message relevant district changes and processes. The power of this existing structure lived in how it offered opportunities for district and school leaders to build their skills, create a centralized message of the district's priorities, and create an avenue to collaborate across the district and school buildings. Further, readiness to address disproportionality varied by district and school leadership from some being ready to lead the work, to others resisting the work, to other leaders perceiving this work was not relevant to them and their school. Some remained convinced that poverty was the central reason for disproportionality in the districts and did not want to consider race. To that end, leveraging existing structures to develop district and school leadership capacity is critical, while centering capacity building for leaders to collectively tackle priority goals and strategies to disrupt disproportionality has the promise to generate impact. Such spaces must also create space for critical self-reflection that engages critical questions on race, equity, CRE, and naming who is most impacted by the current system.

CRITICAL QUESTIONS

1. What are the critical pieces that you are walking away with?
2. How does your district currently use data to address racialized disparities?
3. What does your district do to message the district priorities, goals, strategies, and outcomes?

CHAPTER 4

Years in the Making

Does Having Consistent Leadership Shift Disproportionate Outcomes?

A leader ... is like a shepherd. He stays behind the flock, letting the most nimble go out ahead, where upon the other follow, not realizing that all along they are being directed from behind.

—Nelson Mandela

INTRODUCTION

It was the summer of 2013 when the first author entered a room full of district and building leaders for Palisades City School District's annual leadership retreat. CfD began partnering with the district in the 2012–2013 school year and was tasked with supporting district and building leaders to develop a plan that would address their multiple racial and special education disparities. For Palisades, it included a citation from the Office of Special Education for disproportionately suspending Black and Latinx students with an Individualized Education Plan (IEP), a citation from the Office of Civil Rights for over-suspending Black children, and being identified as a focus district for disparate academic outcomes for students with an IEP, Black, and Latinx students. The meeting started with the district leader stressing that Palisades has a race and racism issue and they would address it. The superintendent had just arrived in the district in the fall of 2012. This moment underscored the tone of the expectations that the superintendent had for leaders in the room, how they would execute their expectations, and ultimately, how the district leader planned to lead the district.

Upfront, Charlie Wright, the superintendent, was able to utilize their clarity, systems knowledge, and vision of how they transformed another district as a leverage point in Palisades. They understood school improvement and employed such know-how by focusing on the areas for improvement that would hopefully systemically shift beliefs, policies, and practices that were leading to disparate student outcomes. Charlie immediately assembled a cadre of external partners to support them and the district in addressing disproportionate outcomes and secured funding to do so. Such partners included an organization that conducted a diagnostic review of the district's special education department. This review offered some of the foundational pieces the district pursued moving forward, including developing accurate data systems and data usage, improving internal capacity to address the needs of various student groups, developing new programmatic systems aimed directly at reducing the academic disparities, and improving the curriculum to align with common core standards. Another partner focused on developing data systems (e.g., assessment, student information systems, etc.) that would be merged into one data system for data utility purposes. To complement such an approach, other partners focused on data accuracy and conducting a comprehensive analysis of what was being done with assessments and data, and alter data usage practices to drive instruction, allocate resources, and drive program improvement. The last partner focused on coordinating partners for a cohesive districtwide systemic turnaround, by targeting professional learning and technical assistance centering educational equity aimed at supporting ongoing capacity in classrooms, both at the building and district level. Further, the superintendent understood that Palisades lacked a strong instructional guidance system and created one through later partnering with a teaching and learning institution to develop literacy and math instructional practices and strategies and to support district and school leaders and teachers. CfD would support Palisades in addressing their disproportionality.

Similarly, the superintendent's vision and prior expertise was a conduit for developing manuals for the School Based Support Team (SBST) process. This process garnered the development of an early warning system[1] and an effort to address the gaps identified by the special education diagnostic review. They further developed guidelines for school and district leadership and an annual critical leadership practices roadmap, including timelines when school culture and climate needed to be assessed and data examined, among others.

Another critical practice developed and employed by Charlie to disrupt disproportionality was using data to both identify where the disparate outcomes persisted, through progress monitoring and evaluation. They would sometimes present academic and behavioral data to the Board of Education using the relative risk ratio,[2] which offers a powerful comparative analysis of risk by student group connected to student outcomes (Klingner et al., 2005). This signaled to the board of education and the greater community that they were centering disproportionality by presenting how the district was performing in this manner. Another notable effort was to recruit more educators that were culturally responsive and invest in hiring new teachers that held less bias-based beliefs (Fergus, 2017).

Charlie had a deep understanding of the ways that district and school leadership are crucial to the success of district and individual schools in achieving equity (Bryk et al., 2010; Fergus, 2017; Khalifa, 2018). Their commitment to working with building and district positional leadership was steadfast through constant investment in their professional learning and technical assistance support. To that end, core to the ways that the superintendent ensured CfD supported their district was through monthly district and school leadership meetings, and school-level leadership equity coaching with all school-based principals and district leaders from various departments. Their expectation was that through this investment in time and resources, the leaders would be able to make changes in their buildings and departments, and hold themselves accountable for the work around disrupting disproportionality (Fullan & Quinn, 2016). The district was relying on the school leaders to turn-key CfD trainings in their buildings, taking ownership of the work by leading disproportionality work, and taking responsibility for their disproportionate data. This chapter contends with: Does long-term superintendency impact shifting disproportionality? In particular, it centers the challenge of addressing educators' beliefs and questions the role of district leadership to create a cultural shift to ultimately impact disproportionality.

DISPROPORTIONALITY AND EDUCATORS' BELIEFS

District and school leaders may not view beliefs (i.e., mindsets) as critical to address disproportionality (Kramarczuk Voulgarideset al., 2021); instead, they solely focus on creating procedures, building practices, shifting policies, and investing in multiple initiatives as the remedy to shift disparities. However, we learned through 15 years of providing training, technical assistance, and consultancy that without also addressing educator's beliefs that live in systems, including deficit thinking, poverty disciplining, color evasiveness, and race-based bias limited shifts in disparities would occur. (Fergus, 2017).

For Palisades, we infer that educators' beliefs and practices impacted their insufficient reduction in discipline and academic disparities. In 2017–2018, the district completed the staff survey (see Chapter 2 for further information). Some of the responses offered by survey participants included beliefs of color-evasiveness and minimizing the role that race played in the disciplinary and academic outcomes in Palisades. More so, as evidenced by the responses below, such beliefs impacted educators' practices.

> I'm tired of everyone blaming race for every problem. Students do not receive enough consequences for individual behaviors and poor attendance. Students and parents are not held accountable for their choices.

> Race is an issue that needs more attention and understandably in an educational setting. We also need to be careful that we aren't creating more of an

issue by using race as an excuse for all negative choices. I have seen an increase in using "race" as a scapegoat for some negative student behavior (academic or socially). Many students are learning that racial differences can allow them to get away with certain behaviors, because then they blame race instead of taking personal ownership of their choices. It is interesting because in the elementary level, students don't immediately jump to race. Adults tend to jump to this concept, but the students are willing to take individual ownership of consequences when they are young. They learn as they grow that their choices can be connected to race and then excused (this is taught to them by adults—whether it is the school systems, parents, or both). Some of the racial divide is coming from "minority" groups themselves. In my limited experiences, I've seen adults/students in minority groups make comments that racially divide more often than I have seen 'white' adults and students make this type of divide. I know we have a long way to go and it's important to move in the right direction. I just want to make sure we aren't making excuses when we could be building character.

These responses resemble educators' denial of the impact of racism and race-based bias on the experience students and families of color were having in Palisades. Further, the lack of grappling and acknowledgment of racism among educators leads them to blame students for the educators' lack of cultural responsiveness, and creates distrust between students and families and educators (Harry & Klingner, 2014). Alongside color-evasiveness, additional beliefs such as deficit thinking and poverty disciplining were prevalent in the district (Fergus, 2017). These beliefs manifest as educators blame poverty, particular communities, parents, and the ways in which they raise their children. In Palisades, such beliefs were prevalent.

The following are additional responses from the qualitative survey responses that reflect additional biases and resistance to centering race in disproportionality. These responses continue to deny the impact of race-based bias and racism on students, families, and communities, instead shifting blame on students and families.

I see many teachers and staff making "excuses" for children based on what neighborhood they are growing up in. They make assumptions about their parents, their early childhood experiences which negatively impact the relationships they are able to build with those students. Many staff members are scared to complete home visits and make an honest attempt to bridge the gap between home and school. On the flip side, many of our families find school threatening. They tell their children not to tell people at school what is going on at home because they may take them away. This disconnect makes it really difficult for families to trust the school system, value our expertise, and find school a safe place to come to for help.

I think often the discussion should be less about race and more about the culture of poverty in America.

I do not see urban school issues as a racial entity. Maybe in intermediate grades and on but not really in primary. The issues in urban schools, in my opinion, only come more from how life is lived in a poor urban city. Education is not valued, teachers/adults/authority figures are not respected. It's difficult to get children to respect you when their parents are telling them that they don't have to listen to you or do what you say.

We need to stop talking about race. That is all we hear about and I am sick and tired of hearing about it. I teach students, not skin color.

When children walk through my classroom door . . . I see a child! To me sex, race or cultural background do not impact how I view the student. Academic work is modified to meet the needs of students who struggle and enrichment work is given to those who excel in school.

I don't think that Black children should be treated differently. It is not right to allow Black children to get away with more just because they are Black. They still have to conform to the norms of the school. I think the issue is black poverty. The other races here are also suffering from poverty, yet can still sit in the classroom and be quiet.

Many teachers don't believe in focusing on cultural or culturally sensitive trainings because they don't see color, which is a problem in itself. Getting those teachers to understand why the discussion of color is necessary and current is the most difficult barrier. In addition, our students of color don't have a teachers of color to identify with and teachers are seen over compensating with "acting black" to make themselves more relatable to our students but are still uninformed and uneducated about what it means to be black in this age and in [Palisades]. Although our schools' behavioral referrals have gone down (especially for boys of color), we still have educational boundaries to overcome. But you can't move forward with teachers who still have bias and blame the children of color for their own failure.

In addition to the qualitative responses in the 2017–2018 staff survey, some of the quantitative results underscored high color-evasiveness with an aggregate value of 4.5 and low levels of culture and racial awareness with an aggregate score of 3 (see Figure 4.1). The color-evasive scale measures educators' ability to ignore students' race. The problem with educators' responding high on color-evasiveness is that it denies the impact of race and racism on students, while blaming students, and scapegoats "fixing students of color," rather than a system (Gorski, 2019). Ultimately, color-evasiveness is a racial equity detour that became an impediment in Palisades. The racial awareness and knowledge scale measures the level of awareness and

Figure 4.1. Perception of Race and Culture: Color-Evasiveness and Racial Awareness Scores

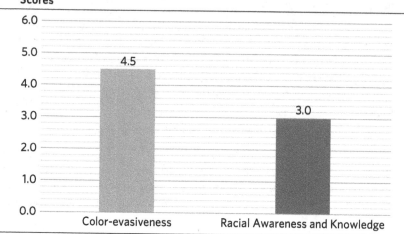

knowledge that staff has about the issues related to race. Further, additional survey questions asked educators about their influence in students' lives, in comparison to home environments (see Table 4.1 for additional survey findings). One of the survey questions particularly asked educators to respond to their influence in students' lives. Forty-three percent of educators agreed with the following question: "The number of hours that students spend in their class have little influence on students, in comparison to their home environment." This finding underscored that educators perceive that student

Table 4.1. Palisades Additional Quantitative Responses

Question	% of Respondent Agreement	% of Respondent Disagreement
If students aren't disciplined at home, they aren't likely to accept my discipline.	50	50
A teacher is limited in what he/she/they can achieve because of a student's home environment.	40	60
The amount a student can learn is primarily related to family background.	26	74
Even a teacher with good teaching abilities may not reach many students.	51	49

n = 436

Table 4.2. Overall Shift in Composition of Behavioral Referrals by Race

	2014–2015	2015–2016	2016–2017	2017–2018	Overall Shift
Black	12,143	13,276	11,646	10,740	–11.6%
Latinx	2,467	4,042	3,983	2,467	0.0%
All Students	21,176	23,275	21,910	19,815	–6.4%

home environments, which are sometimes seen as a deficit (Fergus, 2017), had greater influence on a child's education than the time students spend in classrooms.

To that end, the visioning clarity and expertise that Charlie brought to Palisades, like many districts that produce disparate conditions and outcomes for Black students and other students of color, was unable to sufficiently reduce their disproportionality. We postulate that one possibility for the sufficient lack of progress were educator beliefs. For instance, the overall shift in the composition of discipline referrals between 2014–2015 and 2017–2018 demonstrates an overall decline of 6.4%; the decline varied by student group. Black students received a total of 12,143 referrals in 2014–2015, while in 2017–2018, they received 10,740 discipline referrals, a reduction of 11.6%. However, there was no reduction in the referrals issued to Latinx students (see Table 4.2).

Further, the composition of suspension for all students from 2014–2015 to 2017–2018 increased by 24%. For Black students, the suspension increase was 17.5%, and for Latinx students, the increase was 44% (see Table 4.3).

While the few reductions are important and signaled advancement in improving discipline outcomes, the disparate outcomes still remained prevalent. Palisades was unable to fully resolve being cited by the Office of Special Education for disproportionately suspending Black and Latinx students with an IEP (see Table 4.4). Between 2012–2013 (year 1) of CfD's engagement with Palisades and 2017–2018, the district received a citation for Black, and/or Latinx students with an IEP for indicator 4a, 4b and/or significant disproportionality (see Table 4.4). Further, when comparing the risk and relative risk ratio for Black, Latinx, and all students with an IEP

Table 4.3. Overall Shift in Composition of Suspensions by Race

	2014–2015	2015–2016	2016–2017	2017–2018	Overall Shifts
Black	3,514	3,213	3,464	4,130	17.5%
Latinx	678	922	1,225	978	44.2%
All Students	6,040	5,468	6,291	7,488	24.0%

Table 4.4. Citation Data Patterns 2011-2012 to 2018-2019 Indicator 4a/4b and Significant Disproportionality (OSS>10)

	Indicator 4a (Significant Discrepancy)	Indicator 4b (Significant Discrepancy)	Significant Disproportionality
Notification Year	Suspension Rate	Suspension Rate	Relative Risk (OSS>10)
2012–2013	Overall SWDs–4.90%	Black SWDs–6.77% White SWDs–3.27% (At-Risk) Latinx SWDs–5.50%	No Data
2013–2014	Overall SWDs–4.20%	Black SWDs–5.88% White SWDs–2.28% (At-Risk) Latinx SWDs–5.15%	Black SWDs–1.95 (At-Risk)
2014–2015	Overall SWDs–4.50%	Black SWDs–6.64% White SWDs–2.30% (At-Risk) Latinx SWDs–5.14%	Black SWDs–2.17
2015–2016	Overall SWDs–5.70%	Black SWDs–9.22% White SWDs–2.47% (At-Risk) Latinx SWDs–6.12%	Black SWDs–2.63
2016–2017	Overall SWDs–5.90%	Black SWDs–8.44% White SWDs–4.55% Latinx SWDs–5.70%	Not Cited
2017–2018	Overall SWDs–4.0%	Black SWDs–5.17% White SWDs–2.32% (At-Risk) Latinx SWDs–4.50%	Black SWDs–1.57
2018–2019*	Overall SWDs–YES	Black SWDs–YES	Not Cited

Table 4.5. Risk Index and Relative Risk Comparisons for IEP and Non-IEP Suspensions

		2016–2017	2017–2018	2018–2019
Black Students	Risk Index IEP Suspensions	165.98%	154.31%	93.83%
	Relative Risk IEP Suspensions	2.146	1.576	0.981
	Risk Index Non-IEP Suspensions	118.35%	101.45%	101.42%
	Relative Risk Non-IEP Suspensions	3.153	2.341	1.038
Latinx Students	Risk Index IEP Suspensions	63.98%	104.30%	94.35%
	Relative Risk IEP Suspensions	0.520	0.829	0.991
	Risk Index Non-IEP Suspensions	39.33%	55.01%	90.41%
	Relative Risk Non-IEP Suspensions	0.584	0.845	0.893*
All Students	Risk Index IEP Suspensions	108.96%	120.66%	94.98%
	Relative Risk IEP Suspensions	–	–	–
	Risk Index Non-IEP Suspensions	61.78%	63.05%	98.77%
	Relative Risk Non-IEP Suspensions	–	–	–

and without an IEP, Black students were more likely to be suspended in all 3 years (see Table 4.5).

The district also made less than optimal movement on academic gains for Black, Latinx, and students with an IEP in 3rd- and 8th-grade ELA and math (see Figures 4.2–4.5). While there was some moment in reducing the academic disparities in ELA Proficiency for Grades 3 and 8 over a number of years, Black students, Latinx students, and students with disabilities had proficiency levels lower than the overall student population's proficiency level in the district (see Figure 4.2). The 3rd- and 8th-grade state test math proficiency for Black, Latinx, and students with an IEP mirror ELA patterns with Black, Latinx, and students with an IEP scoring lower than all students.

Figure 4.2. State Test 3rd-Grade ELA Proficiency

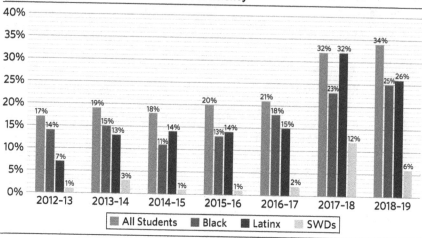

To that end, part of Charlie's challenge in disrupting the disparate outcomes was shifting beliefs that were a result of the racial and cultural mismatch between the student population and educator demographics, particularly teachers and leaders (Clewell et al., 2005; Dee, 2004, 2005; Easton-Brooks et al., 2009; Eddy & Easton-Brooks, 2011; Klingner et al., 2005). The cultural dissonance that is apparent in districts with this mismatch provides a particular set of challenges and resistance when attempting to disrupt disproportionality by propagating a CR-SE approach (Harry & Klingner, 2014). In particular, as highlighted previously through our survey results, we found that many educators do not believe that race and bias-based beliefs play a central role in creating and cementing educational inequities. Thus, with such ingrained mindsets, the lift of improving

Figure 4.3. State Test 8th-Grade ELA Proficiency

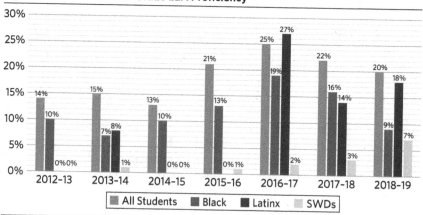

Data is missing for Latinx students for years 2014–2015, 2015–2016.

Figure 4.4. State Test 3rd-Grade Math Proficiency

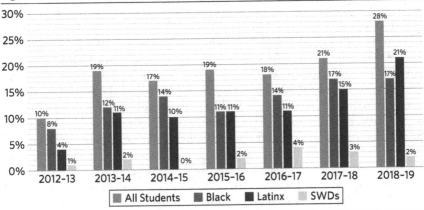

*Data is missing for Latinx students for 2014–2015.

Figure 4.5. State Test 8th-Grade Math Proficiency

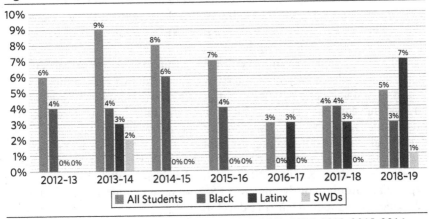

*Data is missing for Latinx students for years 2012–2013, 2014–2015, 2015–2016.

disparate experiences and outcomes of students and families requires a cultural shift. While a superintendent leads, setting the expectations for shifting mindsets, it is not just the lift of a superintendent. It warrants a collective effort among all staff to address disproportionality.

THE ROLE OF A CULTURAL SHIFT IN ADDRESSING DISPROPORTIONALITY: WHAT IS NEEDED?

In addition to tackling bias-based beliefs, for an incoming superintendent, another focal priority is to invest in shifting the old culture so staff gradually change from the old school district to a new entity (Hannay et al.,

2013). Charlie's challenge was to shift a district with a centralized management culture created by the previous administration, in which building and district leaders had to first request permission from the district central administration to make decisions. The shift for Palisades was developing a collaborative culture. The cultures of organizations are formed through past and present experiences. Gruenert and Whitaker (2015) underscore the centrality of culture as fundamental because it reflects the ways that things are done in districts and schools. Culture reflects beliefs that guide behaviors to the point of them being second nature. It defines normalcy and morality held by its members. Gruenert and Whitaker (2015) highlight the impact of six types of culture in districts/schools: toxic, fragmented, balkanized, contrived collegial, comfortable collaborative, and collaborative (see Gruenert & Whitaker, 2015 for specifics). Toxic cultures focus on the negative aspects of the district/schools and staff. Such flaws justify the poor performance of the organization. In contrived collegial cultures, leadership determines how staff should behave; leaders often attempt to speed up the process of school improvement by enforcing collaboration and controlling the situations that foster it. For Palisades, bias-based beliefs were ingrained, shaping the toxicity that students and families of color and students with an IEP would experience. Further, the centralized culture that existed prior to Charlie arriving limited the collaboration of building and district leaders.

Charlie attempted to shift the district culture to one where district, and in particular school building leaders, were expected to make autonomous decisions and lead. For instance, Charlie expected that building leaders have an ongoing data inquiry cycle, including collecting data disaggregated by race/ethnicity, gender, and IEP/non-IEP status, reviewing data, and using data to inform decision-making for their building. Further, leaders were expected to turn-key equity work into their buildings and lead as culturally responsive leaders (Khalifa, 2018). School leaders in Palisades were also expected to autonomously implement School Based Support Teams (SBSTs), adapting the manual the district developed.

However, in Palisades where staff held pronounced bias-based beliefs, and still operated in a centralized management culture, Charlies' deep knowledge in school improvement, experiences in a prior district, and commitment to equity was not enough to shift the disparate experiences and outcomes for Black, Latinx, and students with an IEP. The overhaul for Palisades centered on using knowledge management practices to become a learning organization (Hannay et al., 2013). A knowledge management learning approach requires collaboration between educators, a structure supporting ongoing learning, and individual characteristics, in which mental models are reshaped to increase the capacity to learn. Hence, Charlie needed to be able to create a clear collective vision centering equity and culturally responsiveness—all while ensuring that there was coherence, a culture of learning, and internal accountability (Fullan & Quinn, 2016).

Coherence in this context is defined as a "shared depth of understanding about the purpose and nature of the work" (Fullan & Quinn, 2016, p. 1). Coherence centers the mindsets of individuals and collectively as a system holds a depth of understanding of a district's/school's main priorities, actionable strategies, progress, and results. Internal accountability is central to coherence. It anchors the district so educators connect the purpose of the work. For Palisades, this meant that every stakeholder in the district needed to know about the priorities of the district, the strategies that were being implemented, and had a role in developing and in implementing the district's main priorities (González & Artiles, 2020). One of the main priorities for Palisades was addressing their multiple citations and being a focused district. Implementation strategies were developed around the main priorities, including engaging critical partnerships, having Palisades' Office of Accountability develop data systems and monitor data, restructuring the SBST process, creating ELA/Math curriculum maps, and CfD's involvement in the district, among others.

THE ROLE OF DISTRICT LEADERSHIP IN SHIFTING CULTURE: DID IT WORK?

The Role of Leadership Style and Creating a Culture Shift

A superintendents' leadership style is also important for cultural shifts, school improvement, and racial equity work (Leithwood, 1994), with distributive (Mulford & Silins, 2003), transformational (Mulford & Silins, 2003), and culturally responsive leadership (Khalifa et al., 2016; Khalifa 2018) being primal, and transactional leadership least desired. Distributive leaders inspire a shared vision, model the way by being an example, welcome feedback, and have a clear leadership philosophy. They seek to encourage others by connecting to the heart through acknowledgment and giving recognition (Daud et al., 2015). Transformational leaders create the conditions for leaders and staff bonding that allows for collaboration. This results in a change process that is responsive and innovative, ultimately impacting the performance of the whole organization. Through this process, transformational leaders build shared meaning among members of the district and school staff regarding their purposes of the work and ignite commitment among staff to accomplish these purposes. Such leaders foster norms and beliefs among staff members about the contribution colleagues may make to their practices, including encouraging new ideas and practices, which are all crucial to creating the culture shift that Charlie was seeking. Transformational leaders implement leadership practices that co-create visioning, goals, and objectives, offer support for central stakeholders in districts/schools, and develop distributive structures, and a culture of collaboration (Leithwood, 1994). In addition to enacting distributive and transformational leadership practices, educators must become a culturally responsive leader to ensure that their leadership is culturally responsive and equity driven, and is not color-evasive or deficit oriented. That is, a culturally responsive leader builds important components of "anti-oppressive/anti-racist leadership" (Gooden & Dantley, 2012; Kumashiro, 2000), and social justice leadership to how they lead (Bogotch, 2002; Theoharis, 2007; Khalifa et al., 2016). Such leaders ensure that they learn about the communities they are supporting by reflecting and shifting their bias-based beliefs and becoming critically conscious leaders (Khalifa et al., 2016; Fergus, 2017). On the other hand, transactional leaders do not bind leaders and followers in any enduring way and promote a routinized, noncreative, but stable environment. Transactional leaders are task focused to obtain compliance, and create clarity of roles and tasks required by staff to achieve desired outcomes.

The external accountability challenges in Palisades as a result of being a focus district and having multiple citations required a distributive, transformative culturally responsive leader to lead a system overhaul. This meant it was crucial for the superintendent to build and model a collective anti-oppressive vision that would invigorate all district staff and make explicit connections to how initiatives would support the collective vision (Hannay et al., 2013; Leithwood, 1994; Leithwood et al., 2020). Due to these external accountability measures, Charlie embarked on multiple districtwide initiatives without developing a collective vision alongside teachers, in particular. The absence of teachers and teacher leaders meant collaborative cultures around the purpose of the work were not generated, leading to complacency (Fullan & Quinn, 2016; González & Artiles, 2020). Teachers and teacher leaders needed to be collectively invested and involved in shifting beliefs and practices that chip at racial inequities.

To that end, not all stakeholders were purview to the district's citations and priorities. Not all staff had a shared understanding of the work in Palisades. It is important to note that when individuals have a shared understanding of the purpose of the work, they have a sense of responsibility to improve and will hold themselves, as well as the group, accountable. Hence, this is one of the central lifts of leadership to message the district's priorities (Fullan & Quinn, 2016; Hannay et al., 2013). It was evident that many of the school-based staff did not learn about or know the work that was happening between the district and CfD. In the 2018–2019 school year, the second author participated in the district's strategic planning focus groups across the district; many educators expressed their limited understanding of the role CfD played in the district and how it impacted the district's priorities and their individual practices with students. This highlighted a major gap in the implementation and turn-keying of CfD training at the school building level by building administrators.

The Impact of Centering Leadership Capacity Building, Lack of Collective Visioning, and Coherence

We infer that the lack of collective visioning, initiative fatigue, and responding to the various citations created an absence of coherence that hindered Palisade's ability to significantly disrupt disproportionality. While there were efforts to generate protocols for coherence and a systemic effort for district and school turnaround in Palisades, the depth of understanding and purpose of the work remained with the school and district leadership with limited engagement with teachers and staff. For instance, as a request from the superintendent, the partnership with CfD primarily targeted district and building leaders and focused on building their competency and ultimately, their capacity. Unlike competency that builds knowledge, capacity is the skills of an individual or organization to make the changes required, including the development of knowledge, skills, and commitments (Fullan & Quinn, 2016). The goal of capacity building is to create communities of learners who develop common language, knowledge, skills, and commitment by building vertical and horizontal learning opportunities. This common knowledge and skills must be developed across all leaders and educators in a system focusing on a few goals to sustain an intense effort over multiple years (González & Artiles, 2020; Hannay et al., 2013). As discussed above, the hope of the superintendent was that by centering district and school leadership, they would build their capacity to turn-key and lead equity work. As a result of such an approach that only built capacity with the higher positional leaders, Charlie neglected to prioritize training the body of educators that most directly worked with students.

The engagement of other educators with CfD, including teachers and staff, did not occur until 5 years after CfD began partnering with Palisades. At that point, Palisades engaged in a comprehensive co-facilitated root cause analysis with district and school leadership, teachers, and staff. The assigned CfD associate with a smaller team of leaders met during the summer to develop their capacity to co-facilitate the root cause analysis. The aim of engaging teachers, counselors, and social workers alongside district and school leaders was to build greater internal capacity. Even though a level of capacity was built and the root cause analysis process generated a multi-year plan that was incorporated into the District Comprehensive Improvement Plan (DCIP), the plan was not implemented. We infer that part of the reason the plan was not implemented was the lack of coherence in district priorities, and the lack of offering district and school staff an in-depth understanding of the plan. Further, the plan was not messaged to all staff, including sharing the priorities and the importance of the work (Fullan & Quinn, 2016).

As the work continued to develop, the next phase of the CfD model was to support the principals in the Guardians of Equity work (see Chapter 2 for greater detail) through school-based teams. These teams would include leaders, teachers, and other staff. School-based teams have been proven to support equity efforts by collectively problem solving to shift beliefs, policies, procedures, and practices (BPPPs) (Bryk et al., 2010). Bryk et al. (2010) stressed the importance schools play in improving student learning by using high-quality professional development as a key instrument for change. Maximum results are garnered with a school-based professional community and when teaching is guided by a common, coherent, and aligned instructional system.

To that end, the CfD associate shared research and evidence on the impact of creating teams that center CRE and equity. Charlie agreed to allow school buildings to create teams. While Charlie initially agreed to the idea, they ultimately said that the principals did not need support in the form of teams but instead needed to lead their building in enacting change because that was what they were hired to do. Because of Charlie's stance that building principals needed to lead their buildings, the district effort failed to offer differentiated support for principals (Leadership Institute, 2020). Charlie had "overinterpreted the research of the principal was second (to the teacher) most important source of learning for student" (Fullan & Quinn, 2016, p. 53). It was not enough to continue providing the principal's monthly sessions with CfD. For the principals to be lead learners, they had to model learning alongside their staff (Fullan & Quinn, 2016, p. 54). Targeted support was warranted because principals had different challenges—their own belief and understanding of CRE and equity, their leadership styles, and the role that their social identity (e.g., race/ethnicity, gender) played in advancing the work. Engaging a school-based team was one effort offered to support principals.

Instead of moving forward with the school-based support teams, Charlie began to introduce another problem-solving cycle leveraging improvement science: Plan, Do, Study, ACT (PDSA). While the cyclical nature of the PDSA approach aligned with the GoE protocol, the PDSA problem-solving approach did not center CRE and interrupted a lot of the growth that school building principals experienced through the GoE protocol. For instance, principals began to make connections to actions in their schools and identify policies and practices that they could interrupt that were potential causes of disproportionality. Many of the principals, having to deal with immense responsibility and limited time, had to choose between continuing the GoE goals work and the PDSA problem-solving cycles. School building leaders often had to chose between the PDSA protocol led by the superintendent or the GoE protocol led by the Assistant Superintendent. Charlie received feedback from the CfD associate about the PDSA cycle, including its failure to center race, CRE, and equity. While the superintendent highlighted that the PDSA included a question on race, during the full leadership session, the principals avoided having a color-conscious conversation. Therefore, they did not address the race-based disproportionality that persisted in the district. CfD suggested merging the PDSA process with the GoE protocol because it would ensure that CRE and equity were central to the process. Nonetheless, Charlie did not agree.

As such, power and the positional authority of Charlie played a role in the decision to move away from the GoE process. As the GoE work began to flourish in different areas, Charlie expressed concern about who was receiving credit for the equity work. Charlie told the point person of the GoE work that they thought they were stepping on his toes when it came to the equity work in the district and they wanted the administrators to know that it was they who had made the decisions. Charlie often messaged in front of staff that they were the "equity person" and the work of equity would continue with or without CfD and the only thing that would stop it was their departure.

To that end, at times, Palisades resembled a combination of toxic and contrived collegial culture often exemplified by Charlie's leadership style. These two culture types were present during CfD's engagement. Throughout the partnership the district leader would join most, if not all, of the CfD engagements. The superintendent's involvement was important and demonstrated a commitment to addressing disproportionality and larger inequities in the district. Charlie knew how urgent it was to address the disparate outcomes, and they aimed to speed up the process of having school and district leaders lead racial disproportionality work even while some leaders who were not ready (Gorski, 2019). Hence, Charlie expected leaders to champion the work and hold themselves accountable. They set the ground rules and expectations for leaders and wanted to control how leaders would engage. Such an approach also mirrored their leadership style. At times, the leadership style executed by Charlie resembled transactional leadership. Charlie recognized what employees, in particular district and building leaders, needed and created roles, tasks, a vision, and objectives to achieve the desired outcomes they were seeking (Leithwood & Jantzi, 1990). As such, Charlie sometimes approached his followers with a transaction and obtained compliance from staff in order for staff to minimize their own psychological scarring. That is, over time, district and school building leaders struggled with accepting their role in maintaining the conditions that caused the disparate outcomes, and Charlie began to shame them. For example, in a planning meeting with CfD that was attended by the district leader and their leadership team, they claimed that some of their principals might struggle with addressing disproportionality because of their brain plasticity and their age. In essence, the superintendent modeled to other district personnel that he would make personal attacks if others did not conform or say the right thing. While in some instances their frankness and willingness to challenge educators who were making problematic claims that did not center equity demonstrated his commitment to Black students and other students of color, there were other instances like the one above that minimized that message and instead sent the message to the district that they were willing to shame and embarrass people for not agreeing with them and the work that CfD brought forth. Instead of leading to a collaborative culture, it led to contrived collegial culture and a culture toxicity.

While Charlie attempted to create internal accountability, a sense of external accountability became the norm (Fullan & Quinn, 2016). External accountability is the notion that someone external, like a supervisor, will hold one accountable for one's actions. Internal accountability is more nuanced and complex because it requires the individual to hold themselves accountable for their actions. For many building and district administrators, the district leaders' actions solely created a sense of external accountability. However, the external accountability did not change conditions and outcomes because the accountability was at times a threat of shame and embarrassment in meetings, not through policies that would ensure systemic change. This led to administrators' silence or saying what they thought was the right thing but did not translate into changes at the school building level.

Charlie's leadership efforts to lead the district to equity were commendable. Nonetheless, the cultural shift he was aiming to make was not fulfilled. One potential possibility was not garnering the necessary buy-in from enough staff, coupled with not messaging the priorities of the work and supporting principals in a way that would allow them to bring school building staff on board, thus, not harvesting a collective buy-in and staff ownership. Further, his leadership did not lead to a collaborative culture for staff ownership to occur.

CONCLUSION

Longevity of the superintendent in Palisades was critical. However, shifting a culture, creating collaborative communities, and building coherence are also critical. Charlie's long-term commitment to addressing disproportionality and desires to change the culture of Palisades was central. Further, his clarity, experience, and vision as a superintendent to turn around a district living in the shadows of citations from the U.S. Department of Education Office of Civil Rights, the state Office of Special Education, and being a focus district was important. However, in addition to the expertise and commitment to equity, without developing coherence, collective visioning, a collective learning culture, and individuals holding themselves accountable, such efforts fail to have an impact on addressing disparate outcomes. Charlie had the right intentions and many of the right initiatives to turn around Palisades. He developed partnerships with important partners, secured funding, invested in district and building leaders as central change agents, used data to monitor the progress being made, developed procedures for school-based support teams and leadership, developed a clear vision for turning around Palisades, and messaged the work of disproportionality in different spaces. Nonetheless, during his tenure, he was sometimes impeded by leaders not transferring the work from the training they received to their building and the lack of school building teams to support the principals in bringing these efforts. Further, while some leaders ultimately began to hold themselves accountable for their leadership and role in addressing disparate outcomes in schools, some did not. To that end, the work of improving disparate experiences and outcomes of students and families is not just the lift of a superintendent, it is the work of other leaders to lead, and take ownership, and teachers and staff working collectively.

KEY TAKEAWAYS

The central lessons learned in Palisades on the role of long-term leadership to address disproportionate outcomes include:

Assessing School and Central Administration Leadership Readiness

CfD provided the foundation through training and technical assistance support for the district and school leaders to build competency and capacity to address disproportionality. However, throughout CfD's tenure in Palisades, there was a lot of variation in readiness in school and central leaders to address disproportionality, from some being ready to lead the work to others resisting the work. For instance, some remained convinced that poverty was the central reason for disproportionality in the district and did not want to consider race. Further, this also sometimes resembled school leaders saying, "That is the superintendent's work" and not taking ownership. To that end, assessing school and central leaders' readiness to address disproportionality is primal. This level of assessment can scaffold a support system based on where school and district leaders are and create targeted leadership work based on readiness that centers CRE.

Addressing Bias-Based Beliefs

Disproportionate outcomes will not shift by only creating/revising policies, procedures and practices—bias-based beliefs also need to simultaneously be addressed (Klingner et al., 2005; Fergus, 2017). For Palisades, like other districts that have disparate outcomes for students of color, the bias-based beliefs were endemic. To address such beliefs, districts must develop a CR-SE professional learning plan and develop a culturally sustaining education system (Klingner et al., 2005). Such a system entails assessing, revising and developing policies, practices, and procedures that respond to marginalized student, family, community, and educators' social identity differences. As such, this requires building educators' capacity in CR-SE, grounded in their own personal learning and readiness.

Cultural Shift

Disproportionality cannot be disrupted without an organizational cultural shift. Palisades resembled a contrived collegial culture and a toxic culture. Such a culture did not create the conditions for a true collaborative culture that would create a structure supporting ongoing learning to shift mental models (i.e., beliefs) that would shape local practices. The lack of a cultural shift was coupled by a top-down approach to training and technical assistance advocated by the superintendent. The district leader focused their investment in building and district leadership to shift the district and hoped that such an investment would lead to transforming the district and schools. Without shifting a district culture, districts will remain challenged in building the necessary capacity to address their disproportionality, and shifting their beliefs and practices. As such, district leadership must strategically shift culture by early on engaging multiple stakeholders, making them part of the process of defining the problem, developing the plan to address it, and building their capacity to implement (González & Artiles, 2020).

Building Coherence and Internal Accountability

Central to overhauling a system that dismantles disproportionality, district leaders must develop coherence. Districts who have multiple citations often take on multiple initiatives as an effort to address them without developing coherence. Palisades was a district with initiative overload without coherence. As highlighted above, coherence includes the mindsets of individuals and collective in a system that holds a depth of understanding of a district's/school's main priorities, actionable strategies, progress, and results (Fullan & Quinn, 2016). Coherence is built through collaborative visioning of district and school staff. This offers the opportunity for district and school staff to be part of the process and develop a collaborative culture of committed educators who are invested in ameliorating disproportionality. Through coherence, educators develop a shared in-depth understanding about the purpose of the work, cultivate collaborative cultures, and grow their internal accountability.

Building Multiple Educators' Capacity

In Palisades, the main targets in CfD's trainings and technical assistance support were district and school leaders with minimal teacher involvement.

While leadership is central to change, building the capacity of other staff is also central to overhauling a district with multiple citations. The superintendent had developed a vision for the district; however, to fully execute a focused direction, districts need to build the capacity of staff. While the importance of school leadership is clear, the district needed to provide differentiated and targeted support to school leaders, that moved beyond whole group training and technical assistance from CfD, to build their capacity to be culturally responsive educators. Capacity building across staff creates the condition to cultivate collaborative cultures by developing individuals and groups to execute the work (Fullan & Cohen, 2016). Through this process, a learning organization is developed and mental models (i.e., mindsets) are reshaped (Hannay et al., 2013). Deepening learning is fundamental among collaborative cultures to shape better outcomes.

CRITICAL QUESTIONS

1. In thinking about the role of a superintendent, what are critical focus areas a new superintendent must engage when they have multiple notifications for racial disparities from the federal and state education department?
2. What are potential limitations of only centering district and school leadership for training and technical assistance when addressing disparities?
3. In what ways do beliefs impact movement in addressing racialized disproportionality?

CHAPTER 5

Readiness Woes

District Readiness and Trainer Effectiveness in Addressing Disproportionality

Change will not come if we wait for some other person or some other time.
We are the ones we've been waiting for. We are the change that we seek.

—Barack Obama

CONTEXTUALIZING THE WORK IN HAMSBURG

Hamsburg is reflective of districts needing to start addressing their disproportionality despite not demonstrating readiness. Similar to other districts who are not ready to address their disproportionality, Hamsburg had been cited for indicators 4a/4b for Black and Latinx children with an individualized education program (IEP) (see Table 5.1) and for significant disproportionality, out of school suspension (OSS) greater than 10 days for Black children with an IEP (see Table 5.2). The Center for Disproportionality's (CfD) entry point in Hamsburg was to support them in addressing their citation notification.

The partnership with the district started in 2014–2015 following their participation in CfD's regional training sessions (see Chapter 2). After 2 years of partnering with CfD, the district demonstrated that they were not ready to fully engage in CfD's work. They denied their disproportionality and did not view addressing their disproportionality as an important step in the district. They also did not commit to the number of days and hours of training and technical assistance (i.e., dosage) recommended by the CfD model (see Chapter 2). As such, CfD reduced Hamsburg's support from 27 hours of training and technical assistance in 2014–2015 and 58.5 hours in 2015–2016 to 16 hours of planning sessions in the fall of 2016–2017. For Hamsburg to resume the more robust CfD training and technical assistance service model, they were required to engage in planning sessions and send a team to the 2016–2017 regional training on CRE in late spring to demonstrate their readiness commitment.

Table 5.1. Indicator 4a/4b Citation Notification Patterns (2013–2014 to 2017–2018)

		Year 1	Year 2	Year 3	Year 4
Notification Year	2013–2014	2014–2015	2015–2016	2016–2017	2017–2018
Citation for Black SWD* (Indicator 4b)	YES	YES	YES	YES	YES
Suspension Rate	3.95%	7.03%	6.07%	5.94%	3.74%
Citation for white SWD (Indicator 4b)	At-Risk	At-Risk	At-Risk	At-Risk	At-Risk
Suspension Rate	1.79%	1.73%	1.50%	1.29%	2.20%
Citation for Latinx SWD (Indicator 4b)	At-Risk	At-Risk	At-Risk	At-Risk	At-Risk
Suspension Rate	2.38%	3.15%	4.65%	2.47%	0.80%
Citation for Overall SWD (Indicator 4a)	At-Risk	YES	YES	At-Risk	At-Risk
Suspension Rate	2.40%	2.90%	2.90%	2.60%	2.20%
Threshold for Citation 4a	2.70%	2.70%	2.70%	2.70%	2.70%
Threshold for Citation 4b	3.21%	3.07%	2.98%	3.03%	3.03%

*SWD is in reference to Students with Disabilities.

The CfD associate assigned to Hamsburg became another variable that impacted the overall work. We offer this to acknowledge the implications of not having a district ready to engage the work and how the shortcomings of unskilled trainers and technical assistance providers can impact movement in districts. For the first 2 years of the partnership, the assigned associate lacked an understanding of the CfD training and technical assistance model. They substantially truncated the model to the point that the trainings and technical assistance support were not being implemented as intended. The associate would also subscribe to the requests of the district to change or alter parts of the training and technical assistance model (e.g., condensing root cause analysis process and CRE trainings) without consulting the director of CfD.

Table 5.2. Citation Notification Patterns for Significant Disproportionality OSS>10 days (2012–2013 to 2017–2018)

		Year 1	Year 2	Year 3	Year 4
Notification Year	2013–2014	2014–2015	2015–2016	2016–2017	2017–2018
Citation for Black SWD	At-Risk	YES	YES	YES	YES
Relative Risk	1.91	3.57	2.85	3.41	2.08
Citation for white SWD	NO	NO	NO	NO	NO
Relative Risk	0.49	0.35	0.30	0.30	1.00
Citation for Latinx SWD	NO	NO	At-Risk	NO	NO
Relative Risk	0.96	1.09	1.77	0.93	0.32

The story of Hamsburg stresses the impact of readiness in a district's capability to address their disproportionality. In particular, what does readiness look like for a district that will lead to generating movement in disparate experiences and outcomes for Black children and students with an IEP? Furthermore, this chapter contends with the implications of not having a technical assistance provider who has the capacity to support a district.

READINESS TO ADDRESS DISPROPORTIONALITY

Research has underscored that there are some foundational readiness elements that are needed for organizational change. Organizations need to develop a cohesive group with shared values, a collective vision, and clear expectations of what they are hoping to accomplish (Rushovich et al., 2015). Readiness for change and buy-in from leadership is critical for technical assistance and project implementation (Bryk et al., 2010); when it is absent or weak, it is a major barrier to the provision of technical assistance and project implementation fruition (Rushovich et al., 2015). In Hamsburg, the exiting superintendent agreed to start engaging in work as a result of their citation, even though there was no collective visioning for the work. Moreover, the superintendent did not have a clear expectation of what they wanted to occur. Their desire to "do the work" centered mostly on wanting Hamsburg to no longer be cited; that is, simply being in compliance with the state (Kramarczuk Voulgarides et al., 2021). Even with these red flags, CfD moved forward because the regional partner coordinator shared that they felt Hamsburg was ready to at least start the work.

An additional focus of readiness includes assessing district and school organization infrastructures. School turnaround effort has stressed four domains of infrastructure readiness: (1) turnaround leadership, (2) talent development and management, (3) instructional transformation, and (4) a cultural shift. These domains are used to assess school turnaround readiness in low performance districts/schools and offer specific focus areas of improvement (Hambrick Hitt et al., 2018).

For CfD, readiness to addressing disproportionality was threefold: (1) school district recognizing that race based disproportionality exists in the district and schools; (2) an infrastructure (e.g., instruction support systems, academic support systems) exists in the district to address disproportionality, including systems that are implemented with fidelity; and (3) school and district leaders have capacity to build systems within each of the other school improvement domain supports (professional staff capacity, instructional guidance, student-centered learning climate, and family/community partnerships) to address disparate outcomes (see Appendix G). CfD's readiness tool, highlighting these three domains, offered a gauge of a district's readiness to address their disproportionality. A 0–4 Likert scale ranging from "never" to "all the time" was used, and a composite score was calculated to assess readiness. The scores aligned with a level of readiness criterion. For example, the readiness criterion ranged from *No Awareness* to *Awareness* (see Appendix G). Descriptors for districts who fell in *No Awareness* included the district denying that they had a problem with disproportionality, and perceiving inappropriate classifications and suspensions for certain student groups as part of common practices. The result was a snapshot indication of the district's readiness to begin addressing issues related to disproportionality, and highlighted that tackling their disproportionality would not be a quick fix.

The acknowledgment of the existence of disproportionality in districts was critical. That is to say, "you can't fix what you don't look at" (Carter et al., 2016). Based on the CfD readiness tool, such readiness included where districts scored on their use of disaggregated discipline and academic data, more specifically, how their data was disaggregated by social identity markers (e.g., race, ethnicity). It also included a commitment to having a team consistently addressing the data, and having open conversations around disproportionality, centering race, ethnicity, and language differences as well as culturally responsive practices (Carter et al., 2016). The desired structure to address disproportionality centers on: (1) an equity vision that is shared with school community members; (2) supporting the development and implementation of culturally responsive practices; and (3) monitoring and evaluating the instructional, discipline, and academic support systems that drive equity. Additionally, it is critical that the mission and vision are continuously communicated in all interactions and district improvement plans. Finally, in order to address disproportionality, school and district leaders need to build systems within each of the other supports. This includes: (1) building the capacity of staff to address disproportionate outcomes by training staff in implementing culturally responsive instructional practices; (2) professional learning and coaching offered in culturally responsive practices; and (3) problem-solving teams consistently analyzing discipline and academic data by race, ethnicity, gender, IEP, and ENL/multilingual status. These supports also include (1) instructional support systems that focus on culturally responsive curriculum and materials, (2) a student-centered learning climate that has a clear vision for student and staff culture, and (3) the district prioritizing family and community members as partners in learning (Bryk et al., 2010).

Hamsburg fell short in various areas when the partnership started in 2014–2015, including the failure to acknowledge their disproportionality, and not having an infrastructure in the district to address it. Central to this was the lack of an existing data system to disaggregate academic and behavior data by social identity markers (e.g., race, ethnicity, ability, language). Additionally, systems were missing or inadequate within other essential supports (professional staff capacity, instructional guidance, student-centered learning climate, and family/community partnerships) that are critical to address disproportionate outcomes. For instance, their instructional support system for tier 1 academic support system was limited. This would lead to a tendency to skip tier 2 and go straight to tier 3 (tier 2 to tier 3 signifying more frequent and targeted learning interventions). Hamsburg also did not allocate the needed resources and time for professional learning to remedy this, which became emblematic of the overall lack of time and resources allocated to address their disproportionality.

CfD acknowledges that many of the districts we engaged were not ready to address their disproportionality; however, even districts that CfD ultimately partnered with demonstrated their readiness commitment by: (1) agreeing to the dosage and implementation process of the CfD model; (2) allocating resources to release educators to attend trainings; (3) acknowledging that they had race based disparate academic, special education, and discipline outcomes; (4) demonstrating leadership buy-in; and (5) foundationally understanding it was a long-term commitment, not a quick fix.

CfD aimed to tailor the work to meet districts where they were at; however, overall, the training and technical assistance model was meant to be implemented as intended (see Chapter 2). Over the years, CfD had learned that when the content of the model was truncated too much, it would often fail to meet the intended goals and outcomes, essential to successfully moving districts. For instance, in the root cause process with districts, we learned that when specific root causes and a targeted multi-year action plan was not created, there would be a lack of clarity in how to methodically address disproportionality. Clearly addressing disproportionality included developing priorities, goals, outcomes, and implementation strategies to remedy the identified root causes.

ENGAGING THE ROOT CAUSE ANALYSIS

Training Process Modifications

While the root cause team in Hamsburg expressed excitement to start the work to address their disproportionality, their readiness shortcoming became evident once the root cause sessions were started. Hamsburg had requested that the design thinking approach they had been implementing be built in the root cause training delivery. CfD agreed to this request. However, over time, several modifications were made to the model by the assigned associate because of requests from the district. For example, the CfD model of implementing five root cause sessions, including co-developing the multi-year action plan, did not come to fruition. Ultimately, two team members in Hamsburg alongside the assigned associate met to develop parts of the plan. Further, the assigned associate and a district leader met with mainly school leaders to discuss potential next steps of the plan. The meeting outcome was to implement restorative practices and the district possibly completing the CRE trainings. For a first-year district, only focusing on restorative practice trainings in schools was not aligned with CfD's model. Once a root cause analysis was completed, the first step was creating a systemic, multi-year plan that would center training and technical assistance starting at a district level, and in subsequent years supporting schools. This approach aimed to maintain the work at the district level, while engaging school-level teams in the process, rather than isolating work to schools that ultimately do not lead to the district holding themselves accountable for the work, and developing long-term sustainability. For district level changes to occur, the infrastructural work must start at a district level, prior to moving into school-level work for school-level improvement to succeed (Hambrick Hitt et al., 2018).

Attitude and Belief Baseline

The beliefs and attitudes held by district staff became another critical indicator of readiness. The staff survey offered insight on where the district was in their attitudes and beliefs. A total of 1,061 staff participated in the survey. The survey contains skip patterns for respondents to answer questions that are relevant to them, given their role (e.g., teacher, paraprofessional). The survey result patterns below reflect high agreement on questions regarding color-evasiveness and the denial of the impact of racism, cultural assimilation, and punishment (see Table 5.3). When district leaders and staff struggle with believing that societal and school-based beliefs and structures impact marginalized students, attempts at remedying inequities will continue to fall short (Annamma, 2018).

Table 5.3. Survey Responses

Question	% of Respondent Agreement	% of Respondent Disagreement
I am sometimes suspicious of data showing racial disparities because data can be manipulated to say anything one wants it to say.	60	40
Regardless of family background, schools and classrooms cannot afford to make exceptions to disciplinary policy.	54	46
Tougher disciplinary policies will not solve the disciplinary problems of Black or Latino students.	61	39
Disciplinary action should be taken against students who wear sagging clothes in school.	57	43
Racism would cease to exist if everyone would just forget about race and see each other as human beings.	73	27
Sometimes I wonder why we can't see each other as individuals instead of race always being an issue.	85	15
The things that were done to people of color in the past in this country were terrible, but I am not sure it is the school's responsibility to make up for that.	61	39
I try to ignore skin color in order to view minority students as individuals.	83	17
I try not to notice a child's race or skin color in the classroom setting.	82	18
Trying to be culturally responsive all the time is nice in theory, but the reality is that a teacher does not have time to be all things to all students.	58	42
African American children from disadvantaged neighborhoods do not have the role models they need to be successful in school.	54	46
In a white majority school, Black students are forced to deal with many pressures that threaten their identity as Black students.	27	73
It is important that students of color assimilate so that they can succeed in mainstream American culture.	47	53

TRAINER/TA PROVIDER SKILLS AND DISTRICT
EXPECTATIONS OF THE PROVIDER

CfD's training and technical assistance support centered on building capacity to create sustainable change in districts (Rushovich et al., 2015). This relied on the skill of an assigned CfD associate, including their understanding of their role in implementing CfD's model, their ability to create brave spaces to engage in race conscious conversations that would challenge normative structures of whiteness, navigate white fragility, and build a protective space for marginalized educators. The associate's capacity needed to be highly nuanced to do all of the above. That is, skillfully lean in further to the adaptive work, while still holding fidelity to the technical work. Such expertise needed for implementing the CfD model was grounded in the associates' understanding of their own social identity markers and positionality as it relates to power and privilege alongside more technical aspects such as knowledge of systems change, disproportionality causes and solutions, school improvement, action plans, and technical assistance support. As mentioned at the start of the chapter, it is important to unpack the technical assistance provider capacity to support partnering districts because of the implications it has in districts' movement in addressing their disproportionality (Rushovich et al., 2015).

For Hamsburg, there was a capacity and understanding gap with the assigned associate. The assigned associate was moved to CfD as a transfer from another unit with limited knowledge and skill to execute the work. This included a lack of knowledge of disproportionality, school improvement, and systemic change processes/frameworks. They also had limited understanding of how their social identity and positionality impacted how they would lead and facilitate the work. In particular, how to challenge problematic claims that educators would state about students of color and families and not agree with such claims to get buy-in and approval from educators. Their role was to interrogate such claims through posing questions, and making connections for participants from prior sessions in trainings, and technical assistance sessions. Moreover, the assigned associate oftentimes did not request additional support or consult with other CfD staff and took it upon themselves to make decisions with the district that did not fit CfD's implementation model. As discussed above, the associate made a choice to develop the multi-year plan with two district staff, instead of including the whole root cause team, and made a commitment to instead support schools with restorative practices training. Moreover, they did not request additional help from other CfD staff to support them as they implemented, nor did they inform the CfD Director until close to the end of the school year. Hamsburg went into 2015–2016 without a clear plan on how to proceed. Without a multi-year plan in place, the assigned associate reported that Hamsburg preferred to focus on restorative circles and could not at the time make a significant investment in culturally responsive education. Restorative practices were not the next step of CfDs' model. Culturally responsive education with district and school leadership were the critical next steps. CfD learned from other partnering districts that when restorative practices were not built from CRE, disproportionality in exclusionary practices for students of color would persist. To move forward with some support to the district, the agreement was that the associate and district would ensure the full four-part series of culturally responsive education training would occur simultaneously as the restorative circles training. As such, CfD leadership agreed to support Hamsburg with a 2-day restorative practices training at the high school. However, once the district received the restorative practices training, they discontinued the culturally responsive training. This was another example of the district's desire for a quick fix and not making a long-term commitment to tackling their disproportionality. CfD's leadership expressed their concern to the district for not allocating the necessary time for the culturally responsive trainings. The district leadership reported that they were told by the assigned associate that one session of culturally responsive education was sufficient and they had combined several sessions of the four-part, full-day culturally responsive education into two half-day sessions as a way to build their capacity. CfD leadership explained to the Hamsburg leadership that the two half-day training sessions were insufficient to build capacity and lacked fidelity to CfD's model. CfD's leadership came to an agreement with the district to substantially reduce training and technical assistance support for the 2016–2017 year until they could build a better internal infrastructure and accountability systems that could sustain the CfD services more comprehensively. Subsequently, the technical assistance support sessions led by another associate in the fall of 2016 were mainly planning sessions with district leadership, two train-the-trainer sessions with participants who had been exposed to the truncated culturally responsive education, and support for the equity team that was developed through the root cause process. Hamsburg was also required to send a team to the regional CRE training in late spring of 2017 to resume as a full model partnering district.

(RE)STARTING THE WORK

In the 2017–2018 school year, Hamsburg resumed the CfD training and technical assistance support model, outlined by 96 hours of training and TA. This ultimately led to the district building internal capacity in implementing CRE. The district also developed a strategic action plan centering equity. They further built and started using data systems to monitor their disproportionality, started messaging the work to district and school staff, and focused on engaging families of color.

The first author visited Hamsburg in 2017–2018 when the full-service training and technical assistance model resumed. They met with the superintendent who had transitioned into the superintendency in 2016–2017 after the prior superintendent retired. The purpose of this chapter is not to center the change in superintendency as a reason for readiness, rather to focus on what readiness looks like in districts impacted by disproportionality despite superintendency changes. During this visit, Hamsburg shared their commitment to addressing disproportionality. They moved forward by allocating resources, such as releasing educators to engage in full module CRE trainings. During that year, they trained close to 135 leaders and staff in CRE. They also built data systems that monitored their disproportionality and began using disaggregated data to action plan. They used the culturally responsive curriculum and tools developed by CfD to start reviewing their curriculum for culturally responsiveness. During the associate's visit, the superintendent stressed their commitment to addressing their disproportionality by having multiple district and school staff complete the CRE training, and build internal capacity to implement the trainings with fidelity. The leader wanted to build internal capacity to create the conditions to develop school-level equity teams and districtwide and school CRE practices. They shared that in the next school year, there would be a building leader on special assignment leading the culturally responsive education and equity work.

Small shifts began to emerge from the CRE work with district/school leaders and teachers. For instance, the CoBRAS analysis showed a difference between Session 3 and 4 among 133 participants who were a part of the CRE training with an increase of awareness in racial privilege. Further, the 2018–2019 staff survey qualitative responses demonstrated some shifts in mindsets. The consistent patterns highlighted in the responses spoke to the impact that the CRE training had on educators, identifying ways to apply the training to their practices, and a desire for more staff to complete the training. Staff shared the following:

I have participated in 2 out of 4 days of CRE training. I can see/feel a difference in how I answered this survey in comparison to my previous survey experience. It is imperative that our full staff experiences CRE training starting with "what is race and what is systemic racism." Our small PDs about microaggression and implicit bias were not effective without the knowledge and understanding of the disproportionality issue and the binary nature of race.

Staff at Elms are in a variety of places in their understanding about culture. I do not yet know everything that I wish I did. I am trying to improve my understanding of my own white fragility and the things that I have done that supported the current system that is unfairly treating people of color. This is something that I think is vital for all educators to learn about and improve upon.

We need more educational materials that show minority children in them so the minority children see themselves in the literature and materials they are using.

All teachers need to go through CRE training and not just some educators if we are to have a greater impact.

More staff trained in CRE to help our most difficult staff members to be open to all cultures.

We need more professional development on culturally responsive education. I have worked in other buildings where staff have engaged in this learning for longer.

Once Hamsburg recommitted to addressing their disproportionality, they started demonstrating their commitment in their actions. The district did ultimately assign a building leader on special assignment to lead the culturally responsive education work. The building leader on special assignment primarily took the role of training educators in the district on CRE to build internal capacity. They further trained other educators as co-trainers who would support the training and led additional efforts in developing equity throughout the district. For instance, they led a team of teachers to audit the ELA curriculum for cultural responsiveness using CfD's tool. Over time, Hamsburg trained the majority of their district staff and has since become a primary training site for other districts in their area. That is, Hamsburg has allowed other districts in the area to attend the CRE trainings, and they are now viewed as a leader in equity efforts in their region.

Further, Hamsburg developed a strategic action plan focusing on equity. Their plan started with stressing their district core beliefs. It included honoring the uniqueness of individuals in the school community centering cultural values, orientation, and identities. They further included providing access and inclusivity, and ensuring that every member of the district community was supported. They also looked to operationalize the plan itself through a renewed commitment to key values/beliefs. District coherence was a chief belief. This included building coherence among leaders and staff self-awareness as the foundation for equity, strengthening the district community, and increasing the district and school staff of difference that was representative of students in Hamsburg. Collaboration was another critical belief, including building and maintaining genuine and authentic relationships and centering the importance of differences. These values were connected to five goals, including (1) strong curriculum, instruction, and assessment; (2) empowered staff; (3) engaged community; (4) a safe and healthy environment; and (5) efficiency. On the technical side, Hamsburg also focused on building data systems to track their disproportionality and using data for decision-making. They adopted the usage of the behavior workbooks (see Chapter 2 for more information) in their district and integrated it as part of their practice. The special assignment position for CRE and equity ultimately became the position of director of equity.

CONCLUSION

Hamsburg resembles many districts that CfD engaged with that were not initially ready to address their disproportionality. Such readiness centers on engaging in race conversations and their connection to student experiences and outcomes. Another readiness marker includes not specifically acknowledging their race-based disproportionality, and overall, not having systemic structures to address disproportionality (e.g., data systems that disaggregate by social identity markers). Other districts that CfD partnered with, despite not being ready, did acknowledge their race-based disproportionality, made the necessary commitments to dosage and model to fully engage the work, and allocated resources for educators to be part of the process. In these districts, there was also district leadership buy-in.

Hamsburg's story brings to light the following questions: (1) Should contractors funded by states or federal funds engage State Education Agencies (SEAs) and Local Education Agencies (LEAs) who are not prepared to make commitments to the work even when the contracts are requiring such partnerships? and (2) Should contractors instead spend time first and foremost working with districts who can make a full commitment of time and fidelity to the contractors' model rather than starting the work to begin with? The story of Hamsburg highlights that from the outset, spending time preparing them for the work would have been critical, including assessing their infrastructure, their initiatives, and how these pieces connected to reducing their disparities and developing a vision and goals for the work. Hamsburg also highlights how the capacity of TA providers impacts a district in moving equity work. For Hamsburg, the limited district readiness coupled with the assigned TA provider's limited capacity had clear implications in moving the district forward. This brings to light a larger conversation on the training and capacity that trainers/TA providers need to have to effectively support districts in addressing their disproportionality.

KEY TAKEAWAYS

The following are critical lessons that CfD learned from partnering with Hamsburg:

Assessing Readiness

Current research mainly underscores that readiness is a pre-requisite for implementing change (Rushovich et al., 2015). Limited research exists on assessing districts' readiness to address disproportionality. Often when organizations are contractors of local, state, and federal entities, they are obliged to support districts even though they may not be ready. Hamsburg underscores the implications of not being ready to address their racialized disproportionality. Districts and partners should engage in transparent conversations from the outset when a district says they are ready to address their inequities. In these conversations, it is critical to discuss: (1) the overall commitment to implementing the model of the partnering organization, (2) the allocation of resources and staff time to fully engage in the process, (3) their preparedness to grapple with race-based conversations and outcomes, (4) the potential existing structures to address disproportionality, and (5) the messaging of the work in the district and schools. When districts are not at a place where they perceive they are ready, it may be best to guide a district through a more calculated preparation phase (Blasé, 2009). For instance, this can start with engaging in a book study, having conversations around disaggregated data, and developing a vision and goals for the work.

Fidelity to the CfD model

The CfD training and technical assistance model was intended to be tailored to meet the needs of districts, which is different from changing the core components of the model itself. We anticipated that the model would be adapted based on the district systems, personnel, size of the district (e.g., 6 schools vs. 60 schools), modification on training and technical assistance days, and the technical assistance provider assigned to the district. The goal of the model was still to be implemented as intended, including content, dosage, and process commitment. Nonetheless, exorbitant adaptations occurred in Hamsburg, including not implementing the content and dosage of the root cause process and immediately moving to restorative practice training in one school without having a cohesive and comprehensive plan. It was not just the district culpable for this divergence, it was also the assigned associate, who held a deleterious belief that this was how CfD tailored their work. As such, Hamsburg did not have a plan that would ultimately guide how they would sustainably develop systems to address their disproportionality.

The Capacity of Technical Assistance Providers Engaged in Equity Work

Little to no research exists on the training, knowledge, and skills needed for technical assistance providers to support districts in addressing their disproportionality. The lessons from Hamsburg underscore that it is critical that trainers/technical assistance providers have a highly nuanced capacity to effectively support districts. For the assigned associate, this means having an understanding of their role in implementing CfD'S model, their ability to create brave spaces to engage in race conscious conversations that would challenge normative structures of whiteness, navigate white fragility, and create a protective space for historically marginalized educators. The associate needs to be skilled in understanding how and when to simultaneously alter the adaptive and technical work. Such expertise needed for implementing the CfD model comes with associates understanding their social identity markers and their positionality of power and privilege. Associates also need content knowledge of system change, school improvement, and skills in developing action plans, and offering technical assistance support, among others, to successfully implement the technical work.

Creating a Coordinator/Director Position

While Hamsburg assigned a principal on special assignment to coordinate the CRE and equity work in the district, over time, they created the position of director of equity. Oftentimes, districts add on additional responsibilities to educators to also lead disproportionality work without relinquishing other responsibilities they have in their primary role (see Chapter 6). When a district creates such a position, it demonstrates their commitment to the work, and underscores the role of the director in assessing and monitoring equity in the district. Districts aiming to make shifts in their disproportionality need to create positions for assessing and monitoring equity on an ongoing basis as a foundation for long-term change. This conveys to the district and school community, students, families, and the community at large that a district will make an investment in addressing their inequities, and will have a systemic approach to assess and monitor their inequities. Such an infrastructure creates the conditions for successful equity shifts.

CRITICAL QUESTIONS

1. In thinking through Hamsburg's multi-year process, what were the critical roadblocks to CRE implementation?
2. What preparation has your district engaged in to address disproportionality?
3. Using the CfD readiness tool (Appendix G), what is your district's level of readiness to address their disproportionality?
4. What should be your district's next steps to tackle your disproportionality?

CHAPTER 6

Authorize Yourself

Building District Capacity to Lead the Work

I knew Culturally Responsive Education was my job,
But it put into focus what my work was,
Which is different from my job.

—District co-facilitator

INTRODUCTION

There was a different feeling walking into the CRE trainings in Hayward. Upon first glance, it was much like what you would come to expect from CfD sessions—a group of 25–30 educators, spread out in a drab but organized learning space, with smartboard and various district notices plastered on the walls. However, upon deeper observation, in Hayward, you immediately started to ask questions like, "Who is leading this group?" "Why does it feel like this is such a diverse group of individuals?" and, "How did the group develop such a strong sense of community?" The content connections also seemed deeper because it was clear that the facilitators were largely familiar with the participants in front of them. The questions and feelings that this training space elicited had everything to do with the investment to a CRE capacity building approach in district. The "session leaders" were handpicked district staff who had moved through CfD's CRE training series at least once as participants (some as many as four times at this point due to CfD's gradual release approach), and now as facilitator. The participants were not only school-based educators (e.g., teachers, paraprofessionals, social workers, principals), but also cafeteria and maintenance staff, bus drivers, and central office personnel. During the timeline of these observations, three of the district leaders were training new co-facilitators. There were always three to four "session leaders" and only on occasion did it appear like the CfD associate was one of them. The CfD associate could sometimes be caught whispering directions in the session leader's ear or scrupulously taking notes perched at a side table in the corner. The CfD associate was now in a coaching role, after a multi-year gradual release wherein in-district

Table 6.1. Significant Discrepancy and Significant Disproportionality Citations Under State Performance Plan (Years 2012-2013 to 2017-2018)

Notification Year	Indicator 4a (Significant Discrepancy)	Indicator 4b (Significant Discrepancy)	Significant Disproportionality
	Suspension Rate	Suspension Rate	Relative Risk (OSS>10)
2012–2013	Not Cited	Not Cited	Not Cited
2013–2014	All SWDS–3.70%	Black SWDs–4.76%	Black SWDs–2.54
2014–2015	All SWDS–3.30%	Black SWDs–3.95%	Not Cited
2015–2016	Not Cited	Not Cited	Not Cited
2016–2017	Not Cited	Not Cited	Black SWDs–1.63 (At-Risk)
2017–2018	All SWDS–3.00%	Black SWDs–4.25%	Black SWDs–3.46
2018–2019*	Yes	Yes	Not Cited

*CfD had limited access to state data. CfD did not receive the specific suspension rate due to state contract ending.

staff had developed internal capacity to deliver robust professional learning in culturally responsive education.

While CfD was evaluated and tasked with reducing suspension for students with an IEP, often Black students (see Table 6.1), the best technical assistance is measured by the district's ability to take ownership of the work (Rushovich et al., 2015). District ownership highlights the critical move toward sustainable change. Hayward exemplified this possibility. CfD offered the spark for a culture change that centered CRE and garnered support from the educators on the ground. These educators harnessed the potential to lead their colleagues on their CRE journey so that students of color, in particular, could experience a culturally responsive education that centers a welcoming and affirming environment, high expectations and rigorous instruction, inclusive curriculum and assessment, and ongoing professional learning and support for educators to ultimately shift academic and behavioral experiences and outcomes (NYSED, 2019).

In this chapter, we will explore CfD's Train the Trainer (TTT) model by centering the lessons learned from the associates in the field and their field notes along with the voices and themes brought out through interviewing four out of nine Trainer of Trainers (ToTs) or co-facilitators. Two of the authors of this book who conducted the interviews were overwhelmed by the expressed impact that CfD had on the district. The interview of these trainers occurred in a group that lasted a little over 2 hours. In addition, we will triangulate the interview themes with the current and relevant research on TTT, the district data, and the notes and experiences of the CfD associate(s), two of which are co-authors of this book, to share the important lessons learned from Hayward and the implications it has for disproportionality and larger equity work.

THE SCOPE OF WORK IN HAYWARD

CfD had worked with the district for 5 years. In year 1 (2014–2015 school year), the district completed a root cause analysis that generated a root cause report (see Chapter 2 for more information). The following are some of the root causes, co-identified with the district's Root Cause team, of the district's disproportionate outcomes and inequities:

1. There is a philosophy of punishment operating in the district. There are beliefs that discipline should be punitive.
2. Lack of policy around expectations for instruction. Instruction often is to the whole group (as opposed to more focus on differentiating in smaller groups when possible) and teacher led with usage of worksheets.
3. No equity policy in place, all students get the same.
4. There is a prevailing belief that if families cared about their kids, they'd be more involved in school.
5. There is alienation of families based on cultural differences and expectations.
6. Race-based bias influences expectations of students' success in school.

Due to the identified root causes, the district committed to completing Culturally Responsive Education training starting with central administration and school building leaders.

In the 2015–2016 school year, CfD completed CRE trainings for building and district leaders. Overall, the CfD associate documented that Hayward leaders struggled with owning how they contributed to the inequities that persist in their buildings. At times, building leaders would view the inequities as district based, in particular the distribution of resources, rather than identifying what they were able to control in their respective schools. Moreover, several participants struggled with discussing race and racism.

In the 2016–2017 school year, CfD provided additional Culturally Responsive Education training to four new cohorts. These cohorts included hall monitors, teachers, paraprofessionals, as well as maintenance, cafeteria, and clerical staff. Although there were several tensions and unawareness held by participants in the CRE trainings, like most districts, there were several participants that leaned into the CRE trainings and pushed themselves and their colleagues to consider the role that CRE can play in disrupting race-based disproportionality. At this point, it was clear that the work around CRE was also picking up momentum in the district. However, CfD understood that for CRE to play a systemic role in the district, it would need to move from external partners training cohorts to the district taking ownership of the work.

While there were several amazing participants who wanted to support the district with CRE beyond being trained themselves, the work struggled to become systemic in part because of continuous shifts in superintendents. There were three changes in superintendents in a 5-year period during CfD's involvement with Hayward. Moreover, based on conversations with district leaders, there were minimal shifts in the disciplinary outcomes for Black students. The lack of leadership was so immense that during 1 year of the partnership, CfD was conducting training with no real point of contact in the district. The CfD associate was able to leverage their relationships in the district to ensure the CRE trainings continued despite not having a district-based leader who could make decisions that were necessary to move from training individuals to making systemic changes.

To continue to build the capacity of Hayward, CfD decided to implement a TTT model. The TTT model had the promise of being efficient, cost-effective, and a powerful way of translating interventions from research to practice which can outlive leadership change and uncertainty (Hester et al., 1995; Jones et al., 1977; Parsons & Reid, 1995; Orfaly et al., 2005). CRE Cohort 4 became a critical turning point for the work as it was the first series utilizing a co-facilitation model, where four district staff members, who had already been trained in CRE, co-facilitated the sessions alongside the CfD associate. In addition, three of the four original ToTs began to coach five other ToTs with the support of CfD, through the TTT model. During the last year of work together, the new superintendent appointed one of the CRE ToTs to a principal-on-special assignment to focus exclusively on the disproportionality and CRE work. This decision was pivotal to the success of the TTT model because it ensured that there was a Hayward-appointed point of contact who would work not only on the TTT work but look to embed CRE systemically, further activating what ToTs and participants were learning in sessions. This led to a robust CRE implementation plan and additional school-based support for teachers and school building leaders.

CfD'S TRAIN THE TRAINER MODEL

As highlighted in Chapter 2, CfD's delivery model was created with adult learning theory in mind, looking to engage adult learners by connecting to their lived experiences and developing content that allowed for deep engagement within their communities (Aguilar, 2016; Knowles, 1984; Speck, 1996; Lave & Wenger, 1991). For this reason, the TTT model supported how the CRE trainings were connected to the local context of Hayward. Ultimately, this meant that the ToTs who had lived experiences could connect to what was happening in a way that no external partner could.

To support the ToTs, CfD took on a gradual release approach. First, the district level co-facilitators would participate in the full 5-day training, followed by starting to co-facilitate some content in each training. Coaching occurred before upcoming training sessions often lasting 2–3 hours with the associate and 1–3 hours on their own depending on each individual's own perceived readiness, learning, and preparation style. This pre-session coaching included reviewing the content along with facilitation guides. It is important to note that CfD avoided providing scripts for the ToTs because that often diminished their ability to be authentic in trainings and insert their own experiences and expertise when delivering the content to their colleagues. That said, the facilitator guides would mention key points and core components that needed to be conveyed. In addition, the facilitator guide would mention, where necessary, common reactions from participants to help prepare the ToTs to handle difficult situations and questions regarding racial equity at large. For example, they focused on how to address common pushback that came up around disproportionality data such as when participants' defensiveness and, at times, fragility manifested in comments such as "the analysis here must be wrong!; These can't be our numbers!" The associate was also responsible for supporting the ToTs in deciding which content they were comfortable leading and what content the associate would lead as they would benefit from seeing the material led again. While the ToTs had autonomy to decide what they would lead based on their level of comfort, they were often pushed to try new material knowing that the associate would support them should they feel stuck or unsure during the training. Through this experience, CFD learned that in order to provide this level of coaching, relational trust between the ToT and the associate became critical because while any new learning requires courage, racial equity and CRE work that draws on one's own beliefs and insecurities calls for intensive support to lead.

The CfD associate would then co-facilitate with the ToTs while simultaneously providing immediate feedback, right after their portion is done or during breaks, on the ToT's implementation. Immediate feedback allows the ToT to process the feedback without losing the nuisance or details of their implementation and to address concerns, questions, and the like that come up in the session that cannot always be planned for. In essence, this builds their capacity to address the immediate and local concerns of the individuals in the training. In addition to the immediate feedback, the ToTs would receive and provide feedback after the session was finished, which generally lasted 1–2 hours. This feedback was built into the day to avoid the loss of what happened and the nuances of each session. All the ToTs interviewed mentioned how important this immediate and postsession feedback was for them in learning how to facilitate complex conversations that CfD's curriculum evoked (V. Sanders., T. Giglio., & J. Rogers, personal communication, Jan. 20, 2022). In subsequent co-facilitation sessions, the ToTs would continue to increase the amount of content facilitation they took on. This process would end in the ToTs leading the majority of the sessions with the associate supporting through coaching, feedback, and when necessary, facilitation support if something unexpected occurred or content was inappropriately delivered.

Despite the immense time and effort of the co-facilitation model, in our interview with Hayward co-facilitators, one individual commented that "the model itself was very empowering" (Sanders et al., personal communication, 2022). Several others echoed this sentiment. They highlighted the process of training the trainers as always feeling like it "hit the sweet spot of not totally comfortable but still feeling the growing edge" (Sanders et al., personal communication, 2022). They mentioned that what was cultivated amongst the group of trainers was a "trusting environment to be vulnerable" and that there was a certain level of trust "in process and in people" (Sanders et al., personal communication, 2022). CfD focused on building this collaborative culture (Fullan & Quinn, 2016) through continued relationship building—which was indeed a skill of the associates[1] assigned to the districts—and also through an adherence to an approach to coaching and providing ongoing support and feedback.

BUILDING INTERNAL CAPACITY AND ACCOUNTABILITY

In CfD's work with districts, the communication between district leaders and district educators often felt like top-down mandates, particularly because this work was sparked by an IDEA state citation—an external accountability measure that could feel very much disconnected from the teaching and learning happening in classrooms. As districts attempted to address their disproportionality through initiatives such as restorative practices (RP), Positive Behavioral Support Systems (PBIS) and other research- and evidence-based practices, teachers and building leaders constantly were feeling initiative fatigue—a level of exhaustion in all that is being asked of them (Kuh & Hutchings, 2015). CfD noticed similar initiative fatigue when completing CRE training, which often was introduced as an add-on to the already overwhelmed reality of educators. This can immediately limit any potential success for implementation and growth.

In essence, culturally responsive education training—and any "equity training" for that matter—more often than not lives in districts and schools as "initiatives." These initiatives then become messaged to educators as the next thing teachers need to do in their classrooms. One of the main reasons so many of these "equity initiatives" never develop roots lies with the fact that the accountability structures messaging the work focus on external accountability rather than cultivating internal accountability (Elmore, 2004; Fullan & Quinn, 2016). Fullan et al. (2015) defines internal accountability as "a collective commitment and responsibility to improve student learning and strengthen the teaching profession." One of the ToTs mentioned the importance of this shift: "This is Hayward and [CRE is] one of our core beliefs" (Sanders et al., personal communication, 2022).

CfD's approach moved beyond seeing CRE as an initiative or add on. Instead, CRE was the foundation to equitable schooling through changing the conditions and experiences that marginalized students often experience in our school systems, especially those cited for disproportionality (Klingner et al., 2005). ToTs were trained to address this concern and often used the metaphor of CRE not being another add on to an already full plate but CRE was the plate itself. This would ultimately be the paradigm shift districts needed to take on. This meant that all other areas of our educational system needed to be culturally responsive. For example, if the district was going to adopt PBIS as their behavioral system they needed to ensure they were implementing a Culturally Responsive PBIS system (CRPBIS)[2] (Bal et al., 2012) or if they were attempting to increase the diversity of their teaching workforce, they would need to make their hiring process is culturally responsive and equitable while aiming to hire culturally responsive educators (Warner & Duncan, 2019).

Addressing how CRE is perceived by the district and its staff is important to building internal accountability especially for the ToTs. Over time, the core group of Hayward co-facilitators, led by CfD associates, fostered a culture of collaboration and internal accountability (Fullan & Quinn, 2016) that moved the work of CRE from an CfD initiative to a Hayward core belief and approach. Through the training of nine consecutive district cohorts, the process no longer relied on a mandate or external directive, but began to live with the accountability mechanisms developed and maintained by the core co-facilitation team. Due to the strategic selection of trainers and participants, accountability was spread far more horizontally, rather than from just those with positional power in the district. CRE was no longer just a response to a state citation but a foundational approach to teaching and learning that inevitably started to transform and impact pedagogy. For example, when asked how the work of the CRE cohorts impacted school-level practices, one of the co-facilitators highlighted that "teachers you wouldn't expect to notice inequities, started to notice—microaggressions, inequality, disproportionality" (Sanders et al., personal communication, 2022). This growing awareness and understanding becomes the bedrock for more welcoming and affirming environments, particularly for marginalized students and families (NYSED, 2019). It becomes the means to shifting policies, procedures, and practices. You can only change what you know, so it becomes critical to highlight the practices and everyday actions that lead to disproportionality.

SELECTION OF THE TRAINER OF TRAINERS

To support building the internal accountability of the district, the selection of the ToTs was crucial to the process. As CfD moved through the first year of CRE training, four key district employees demonstrated their commitment and desire to continue being *lead learners* (Fullan & Quinn, 2016) and take on more responsibility in spreading CRE throughout district buildings. Fullan and Quinn (2016) assert that lead learners "build professional capital across organizations by modeling learning, shaping culture, and maximizing the impact on learning" (p. 54). One individual, who inevitably led, grew, and transformed the CfD CRE model, was a building principal at the time—later transitioning into *principal on special assignment* to solely focus on CRE training and district CRE support—the second was a home-school coordinator, the third operated as a director of ENL and Refugee services, and the fourth was a school principal; the fourth ToT did not stay on for the duration of the TTT due to personal issues and retirement. This group had reach—they had inroads in district offices, school buildings, and family and community outreach to really shape the culture of the district. They spanned varying social identities—a Black, Muslim female, a Black male, and two white males (only one was able to continue) all of whom were cis-gendered. As they grew their own team of trainers,[3] they looked to create an even broader representation.

Three of the ToTs co-facilitated CRE training while simultaneously supporting new ToTs using CfD's TTT model with the associate's support. The new ToTs represented a diverse set of roles and identities that were more representative of districtwide roles, responsibilities, and social identities: A white male who directed the district maintenance team, a Black male assistant principal, a Black male home school coordinator, a Black, Muslim female teacher, and a white female, all of whom are cis-gendered, stepped into the ToT process and began cofacilitating sessions. With this growth came greater access to individual schools and district offices. Each of these individuals fostered deep relationships in the learning communities they were a part of. They used these relationships to help identify the future cohorts that would be trained—focusing again on racial, gender, role diversity, and readiness of the potential ToT candidates.

It became critical to engage all building leaders in the district whether they participated in the CRE trainings themselves or not. The principal on special assignment who led the effort began to identify and cultivate building-level equity teams. By the end of CfD's partnership with Hayward, they were utilizing their "on-assignment" role to observe and support CRE practices in buildings throughout the district, while still running cohorts and leveraging other ToTs to share their learning. For that year, having a district-appointed role became very meaningful. It was both a recognition of the immense workload of coordinating and leading the CRE cohorts as well as a signifier that the district was investing in the work. That said, they found themselves up against district policy and procedural challenges to continue the work, which inevitably became one of the key barriers for even deeper systemic growth as mentioned later in this chapter.

THE ROLE OF THE CfD CURRICULUM

Several Hayward co-facilitators commented on the strength of the CfD curriculum as a key mechanism for the trainers' and participants' continued growth. Central to this was the material being comprehensive and deeply researched. As one of the ToTs mentioned, having a well-researched curriculum for all of the CRE session content slides offered a strong foundation for trainers to feel supported and feel like the learning was active and ongoing (Sanders et al., personal communication, 2022). As they prepared for sessions and needed more grounding in a particular content area, they could always look to one of the many research citations for support. Moreover, CfD associates looked to drive home that the content in the curriculum was there to support the learning and the learning itself had to be malleable and dynamic. That is, if the group was struggling to understand microaggressions, trainers needed to take more time and lean in with this particular content area. In addition, the curriculum "allowed us [the ToTs] to authorize ourselves to add pieces like current events in the district" (Sanders et al., personal communication, 2022). The "allowance to customize" was a critical learning point for Hayward. This "allowance" then became ownership by empowering the ToTs to authorize themselves to customize and tailor the training while not losing the core components of CRE (Sanders et al., personal communication, 2022). CfD associates would often highlight this approach to learning as a model for how we think about our work with children—using content to engage ideas and spark dialogue and move through tensions and discomfort as opposed to numbly skating through standards without making the deeper connections that create true growth. In essence, CfD aimed to model best practices of teaching that are also culturally responsive to participants of the CRE trainings. CRE is not and should never be task-laden work, checking off boxes as individuals move through content areas to get to an imaginary finish line.

ONGOING CHALLENGES

As mentioned in Chapter 2, CfD underscored the importance of leadership in school improvement efforts (Bryk et al., 2010). If leadership is indeed a critical lever for systemic change, what becomes the impact of having three different superintendents in 5 years? In most cases, districts continue to cycle through popular initiatives, started and stopped by the revolving door of new district leaders. Priorities and messaging continue to shift and buy-in for foundational work can easily start to wane due to changes in leadership compounded by initiative fatigue. However, because of the relationships built by the associate assigned to Hayward, the IDEA citation, and an investigation from the state's attorney general for over-suspending Black children and students with an IEP,[4] Hayward was able to maintain a foundational connection to CRE amidst the changes. Through the strategic selection of participants and trainers, a core DNA persisted. That said, Hayward still was not immune to the impact of leadership change.

At best, with each new superintendent transition came a new jockeying for recognition—recognition of the critical importance of districtwide CRE training and CRE-based district policies as well as the recognition for the sizable lift inherent in moving the work. At worst, a superintendent may not want to continue the work of CRE. The ToTs and many Hayward staff that had participated in the trainings had experienced the gradual impact of building coherence across buildings and most importantly, the positive effect CRE practices, such as including students' cultures into lesson plans, were having on students and educators. At the end of the CfD partnership, there was a palpable feeling of unease with where CRE fit in the overall district approach to teaching and learning. Some of the CRE training participants even expressed that they were unsure what the district's leadership vision was for CRE, which spoke to a lack of coherence in the district at that time. One ToT mentioned that it felt as if "we moved the goalposts past where folks in the district were ready" (Sanders et al., personal communication, 2022). There was a new superintendent who was clearly passionate about school equity, but had not gone through CRE training and was not able to fully understand the scope of what had already taken place in the district. Just like other superintendents who struggle with seeing CRE as foundation to all initiatives, they did not have the understanding of CRE as the "plate" or foundation for all initiatives and undergirding approach to teaching and learning. Instead, the new superintendent saw CRE as another initiative, alongside programs like *My Brother's Keeper* and PBIS. The momentum that had developed over multiple years of district trainings gradually moving into school-level equity teams and school-level capacity was at risk of slowing down. This leader misunderstood that equity was what the district wanted to achieve and CRE was how they would achieve it. Instead, they pitted equity and CRE as something different and as competing ideas.

Additionally, the tension of time and compensation was always present in Hayward. As mentioned earlier, the ToTs were attending 5 full-day training sessions with each necessitating approximately 4 to 6 hours of preparation and debriefing. How could the district recognize and provide resources for the work co-facilitators are doing with the CRE training cohorts? As one co-facilitator mentioned, "The CRE co-facilitation preparation takes a great amount of time to prepare and there were no allocated times for the facilitators to build their capacity during the work day" (Sanders et al., personal communication, 2022). A few members of the core facilitation team recognized this work was more of "a calling" than a profession and because of this they knew that they would invest their personal time either way, but would have, at bare minimum, appreciated the recognition (Sanders et al., personal communication, 2022). CfD worked with other partnering districts that financially compensated participants and CRE facilitators through the use of district-based per diem rates, recognizing the importance and difficulty of balancing their district roles and the lift of learning and leading new CRE competencies. This would have been an immensely impactful step in Hayward.

CONCLUSION

Hayward represents the potential of what an effective TTT model of CRE training can look like. That said, Hayward never saw its full potential due to ever changing leadership, which contributed to a lack of coherence around centering CRE (Fullan & Quinn, 2016). While this particular district was a beacon of hope and success, unfortunately there were pitfalls that never allowed Hayward to experience the success that it could for the children and communities it has marginalized decade after decade, as evidenced by IDEA citations for Black students with an IEP and the attorney general's involvement for the over suspension of Black children and students with an IEP.

For the TTT model to be effective, it had to move beyond what the individual ToTs or the participants of the training were gaining. If the TTT approach is solely evaluated through what ToTs and participants gained, the district may feel like they are in a forever cycle of long trainings that shift individual beliefs and practices but never disrupt the systemic inequity. There were Hayward staff who wanted and believed CRE was foundational to their work but in the absence of a coherent district wide plan supported by district leadership were disillusioned by the district. In fact:

> Having a moral imperative doesn't mean much if you are not getting somewhere. In the absence of progress, educators lose heart—or never develop it in the first place. Of course, some do maintain their moral drive, but it is against all odds. Humans need to experience success to keep going; they need to understand and experience the conditions that advance the cause. In many situations, constant overload and fragmentation overwhelm moral purpose. (Fullan & Quinn, 2016, p. 17)

While CfD advocated and, at times, were successful in attempting to support the district in adopting a coherent plan, especially the one developed by the principal on special assignment, it was limited to the direction of each new superintendent or lack of superintendent involvement.

Despite these shortcomings, Hayward was left with hundreds of staff that were trained and could implement their own practices at all levels of the district. As one of the ToTs mentioned in our interview, "CfD left a legacy in the district that moved CRE from being a part of the conversation to being *the* conversation" (Sanders et. al., personal communication, 2022). As we focus on systems change, it is imperative to continue to honor the power and dedication of the individual ToTs in Hayward and their ability to lean in and create shifts in a culture amidst all barriers.

KEY TAKEAWAYS

The central lessons learned in Hayward regarding a TTT model for CRE include the following:

Investing in the CRE Train the Trainer Model

Districts must make a human, financial, and time commitment to developing an effective CRE TTT model to address disproportionality and other inequities. While we saw great potential with the TTT model in Hayward, the financial and time constraints can make it difficult to implement the model. It is important to note that there was no cost of having CfD because the state grant covered these costs. However, it was critical that districts budgeted for additional resources (e.g., teacher substitutes) just as they would should they look for outside consultants through a Request for Proposal process.

In addition, as we learned with Hayward, it is imperative to have a consistent point of contact who is committed to the work and has positional authority to make decisions. Hayward moved beyond this by investing in a principal on special assignment whose job was to lead the TTT model and support schools in implementing CRE.

Investing in the Trainers of Trainers

Understanding disproportionality and the role of race and racism is complex and nuanced work. In Hayward, there was immense professional learning and technical assistance provided to the ToTs. They participated in the CRE trainings before being gradually released to fully lead the trainings. CRE requires the building of one's own sociopolitical and critical consciousness (Ladson-Billings, 2021), understanding one's own racial identity development (Tatum, 2013), deeply understanding CRE (Ladson-Billings, 1995a, 1995b, 2021; Gay, 2000; Paris, 2017) and imbedding the belief changes into policies, procedures, and practices.

CRE Is Not a Quick Fix

This model is not a quick fix and must be supported with additional policy, procedural, and practice changes at the district and school level that center CRE. Hayward began to see shifts in practices as the ToTs, and in particular the principal on special assignment was able to provide embedded school support. The trainings in and of themselves did not create the necessary change to disrupt disproportionality.

CRITICAL QUESTIONS

1. What steps can your district leadership take to invest the human, financial, and time commitment toward an effective CRE TTT model?
2. Is there a leadership position and/or office designated to support the CRE work? If not, can one be created?
3. What resources may need to be allocated to implement the TTT model?
4. Is there a multi-year, systemic approach in the district to implement the CRE TTT model?
5. Is there enough bravery in the district to stay the course and address resistance?

CHAPTER 7

From Self to System

Attacking Disproportionality Through Culturally Responsive-Sustaining Education

If your success is defined as being well adjusted to injustice and well adapted to indifference, then we don't want successful leaders. We want great leaders who love the people enough and respect the people enough to be unbought, unbound, unafraid, and unintimidated to tell the truth.

—Dr. Cornel West

WHERE ARE WE AND WHERE DO WE GO FROM HERE?

We opened our book with a glimpse into a training and community space rife with racial tension, power struggle, and a continued maintenance of the myth of white supremacy. Across the country, racial disproportionality continues to exist in outcomes and experiences within these contexts. Students of color are continually excluded, pushed out, or forced to assimilate into white normative culture, by which value is given to an individual's and community's proximity to whiteness. The re-enactment of the Individuals with Disabilities Education Act (IDEA) prompted greater enforcement from federal entities for states to address disproportionality in disciplinary outcomes and enrollment into special education (IDEA, 2004). However, the vast majority of approaches have been surface level or misguided (Kramarczuk Voulgarides et al., 2017). State departments have calculated a district's disproportionality, sent off citations, and sometimes connected with technical assistance support to attempt to respond to the inequitable outcomes. Many districts that the Center for Disproportionality (CfD) interacted with were cited for several years in a row (and some for as many as 13 years in a row) prior to formally addressing their disproportionality. Direct action and long-term implementation to dismantle systems leading to disparate outcomes continue to fall short. During CfD's 15-year existence, the organization strengthened its focus on interrogating the beliefs held by school systems and maintained by educators and leaders as well as the policies implemented through practices. Decades of research coupled with a tremendous amount of experience in the field, directly partnering with 75 districts and offering regional training to 70 additional districts, reinforced the fact that school-based inequities continue to persist without foundationally addressing beliefs (Fergus, 2017). Regardless of the variation in the student, staff, and community demographics of CfDs districts, certain things always rang true:

- We don't get to equity without acknowledging and eradicating the beliefs that lead to historically marginalized students, particularly Black, Indigenous, and Latinx, being punished, excluded and offered less humanity than their white counterparts.
- We don't get to equity without recognizing how deficit thinking bleeds into school policies, procedures, and practices.
- And we certainly don't get to equity by maintaining a color-evasive lens and failing to acknowledge and understand how race and racism continually impact students and families of color, in society, and more specifically, within the walls of our classrooms.

The work of CfD almost always felt like swimming upstream. Grounding the approach in culturally responsive education (CRE) meant believing that the everyday push lived with an adherence to a *pedagogy of opposition* (Ladson-Billings, 1995). Training and technical assistance providers seldomly take on this foundational, everyday position and instead enter spaces and seek to make existing systems more efficient (Kozleski & Artiles, 2012). TA and training around disproportionality must seek to uproot, disrupt, and dismantle existing oppressive beliefs, policies, procedures, and practices (BPPPs). Our youth have always known this to be true. The Youth Center for Disproportionality (YCfD) reminded us of this each and every time we had the privilege of working alongside them, defining disproportionality as the outcome of institutionalized racism and bias. While CfD sometimes struggled with always holding the nuance of this foundational push to dismantle disproportionate outcomes and experiences—as we will further acknowledge in the "Lessons Learned" section of this chapter—it did become the prevailing belief and a central part of the theory of change for the director and associates who closed out the CfD contract.

Fighting for a more equitable school system started with leading by example and fostering an environment within training sessions that reimagined the way we create culturally responsive learning environments for students, families, and educators. At its best, CfD's work was grounded by the following guiding questions:

1. *How do we hold space in our sessions for colleagues, families, and students of color who have continually been fighting this battle?*

During CfD training sessions, educators and parent/caregivers of color often shared stories about being gaslighted by white school leaders and teachers—feeling invalidated and dismissed when sharing the reality of their experience as a person of color fighting to promote equity in the district. These examples continued to highlight ongoing harm committed by white educators who had not done enough personal work to recognize the impact of their own whiteness. Honoring and acknowledging the history of racism in the United States starts with holding space for this reality within the walls of our classrooms, district buildings, and professional development sessions. CfD always sought to bring these realities to light within sessions, naming who continued to carry the burden of racial disproportionality work and challenging participants to reckon with this reality.

2. *How do we challenge and aspire to cultivate a brave space with white participants by not coddling them, but rather, naming where fragility and defensiveness aim to derail progress?*

Being able to "hold space" for participants of color is only possible if facilitators are able to call out and challenge the ways in which white supremacy culture consistently impedes racial justice progress. Effective training that centers race and racism and pushes for culturally responsiveness inevitably breeds deep emotions. White participants bring particular baggage into sessions that, without fail, comes with feelings of anger, vulnerability, shame, and white guilt (DiAngelo, 2018). As we look to dismantle racial disproportionality and move equity and racial justice work forward, Audre Lorde (1997) provides context for how we must engage the emotions of white participants in particular:

> Guilt is not a response to anger; it is a response to one's own actions or lack of action. If it leads to change then it can be useful, since it becomes no longer guilt but the beginning of knowledge. Yet all too often, guilt is just another name for impotence, for defensiveness destructive of communication; it becomes a device to protect ignorance and the continuation of things the way they are, the ultimate protection for changelessness. (p. 280)

The nuance in this push becomes critical, because the goal continues to be systemic change and not simply the unpacking of individual bias and the dwelling in white guilt and white tears. Amid research on the potential ineffectiveness of equity trainings that focus exclusively on the beliefs held by participants (Mehta, 2020; Dobbin & Kalev, 2018; Guskey, 1985), Lorde's push for action by moving through defensiveness becomes critical. CfD looked to realize this balance through a focus on both the adaptive and the technical work (outlined further in the CSC Theory of Change). More tangibly, it became common practice for associates to ask questions like, "Has white fragility shown up in our sessions?" "How?" Moreover, when white participants were actively defensive during particular dialogues, CfD associates were expected to challenge them and unpack whatever tensions were being held. One longstanding CfD director would commonly say, "You can't leave that in the room" during debriefs with associates and co-facilitators. If it's not engaged and challenged in training spaces, we won't see a change in our classrooms.

> 3. *How do we shift the paradigm of who is offered "full humanity"*
> *by modeling it inside of our training and TA sessions in effort*
> *to reshape the learning environments being cultivated in our*
> *classrooms and with our students?*

Inevitably, as culturally responsive education trainers, the modeling of holding space and holding accountability is not just to build the capacity of the participants in each training, but most critically, to ultimately shift what is happening in classrooms with students. How do we move past intent and into a deeper understanding of the impact schooling is having on our marginalized students? In training and TA sessions, so much of the modeling needs to center on *how* we talk about our students and *whose voices and experiences* we uplift. The data continues to paint a clear picture of who is offered humanity in our schools, who benefits from being *fully seen* and who continues to be othered and disproportionately impacted. Our educators also need to experience a more inclusive and culturally responsive space for themselves in order to reimagine the learning environments they seek to foster. During sessions, dialogues around exclusionary discipline and the uniform policies pushed participants to reflect on who is given full humanity in their schools. These conversations inevitably connect personal history and belief systems with the ways in which we engage our students. Often similar questions to the following were posed: If we are treating everyone the same, why are Black students 4 times more likely to receive a suspension for subjective reasons? Why can't the school with almost all Black and Latinx students wear hoodies but the predominantly white school can?

Using the above three overall process questions as additional filters for success in trainings became central to the work of CfD—work that is rarely crystallized on paper or in a PowerPoint and is cultivated from countless hours in the field offering training and technical assistance to a wide range of partnering districts and regions.

LESSONS LEARNED

Each case study that we have offered in this book was reflective of consistent scenarios that CfD encountered during the 15 years of offering state technical assistance support. We learned how districts would engage and resist the work (see Table 7.1). As disproportionality continues to impact schooling experiences and outcomes across the country, we look to offer key takeaways that can support the continued fight to disrupt and dismantle systems that disproportionately impact marginalized student populations. When thinking about comprehensive support to do this work, we are continually reminded that technical assistance cannot live by itself—it has to be accompanied by robust professional development and training. Training and TA as separate entities leads to a lack of capacity building. Equity efforts are ongoing and based on everyday actions and because of this, providing consultations and TA to district and school leaders when issues come up can be critical to developing and sustaining a culturally responsive system.

For example, district- and school-based leadership spends a significant amount of time responding to family and community concerns that inevitably come up throughout the school year. Due to the nature of schooling in the United States, these concerns are frequently about students of color not feeling welcomed and affirmed in their classrooms and parent/caregivers imploring the district to be more responsive. Unfortunately, we noticed that leaders often respond with defensiveness and inaction. A CfD intervention and TA support in these scenarios would bring the dialogue back to thinking about creating a more culturally responsive system, in this case, talking through protocols and new mechanisms for supporting family and student voice in the district. For some districts, this would mean supporting the design of a district equity committee where parent/caregivers hold a leadership position. In other districts, it might take the shape of walking through steps to develop a districtwide student group focused on equity. In any case, having ongoing TA support that is grounded in CRE training and content becomes critical for districts.

Over the years, we have also reinforced our belief that we must move beyond special education outcomes and focus our equity analysis starting with general education to identify the foundational root causes for disproportionality. It has long been the practice to take band-aid approaches to systemic cracks in the foundation of public education. While surface level changes may result in minor shifts to disproportionate assignment in special education, we know that the process of developing welcoming and affirming learning spaces for *every* child starts with general education and tier one academic and behavioral systems of support. Tier one systems become the universal teaching and support that is offered to every child in school. School buildings need to take a closer look at the cultural responsiveness of this foundational layer of instruction because students are all too often moved into special education tracking without first assessing whether the interventions they are receiving are taking into account variations in learning based on cultural differences (Harry & Klingner, 2014). How are students of racial/ethnic/cultural difference being treated in the cafeteria? In school hallways? What kind of differentiated instruction is happening for students that aren't part of the white normative culture? What happens the moment our children of color walk through the doors of a school, well before they have been pushed into a tracked system from which they may never disembark?

Overall Lessons of Engagement and Resistance to Addressing Disproportionality

We want to highlight the patterns of engagement and resistance that we noticed throughout our tenure with partnering districts. We learned that it was critical to understand how districts engaged/did not engage and resisted/did not resist the work and the ways these responses had an impact on their overall effectiveness in addressing disproportionality. Alongside our noticing in the field, the 2017–2018 CfD' evaluation report identified critical indicators of engagement and resistance in CfD districts. These indicators included logistics, buy-in, dissemination and follow-through, and attitudes and beliefs. Logistics focused on districts allocating resources to engage in the work, including releasing educators for training, resource allocation (e.g., a designated contact person for the work, meeting spaces), responsive communication, and commitment to scheduling the work and number of days needed. Buy-in included the degree that participants were willing to and desired to engage, learn, and implement lessons from the training. This included their consistent attendance at trainings, being prepared for the training (e.g., completing the assigned readings/tasks), and being a champion of the work. It was critical that leaders demonstrated their buy-in with action for other staff to feel the work is important. Dissemination and follow-through focused on the next steps participants took once they left trainings. This included messaging the work in the district and schools, including sharing citation data and overall support of implementing the scope of work. We often found that attitudes and beliefs could be indicators of resisting the work. Demonstration of participants' attitudes and beliefs included not seeing the value of the trainings, resistance to discuss race, complacency with the district citation, denying disproportionality, and challenging and attempting to recalculate the data.

The entry point in Table 7.1 represents where districts were at the start with their engagement and resistance. The midpoint is in reference to how districts moved once training and technical assistance took place. The endpoint was where districts were once CfD left. It is important to note that these are anecdotal noticings that we observed with several districts. Table 7.1 offers examples of consistent patterns of resistance and engagement with districts.

Table 7.1. District Patterns of Resistance and Engagement

Entry Point	Overall	– Wanting a quick fix
		– Request for names of other districts who had "fixed" their disproportionality
	Logistics	– Not committing to the number of training/TA work days
		– Request to modify CfD work
		– Not allocating resources to release participants for trainings (e.g., substitute teachers)
	Buy-in	– Participants not consistently attending sessions
		– Most participants not prepared for trainings
		– Leadership not championing the work
	Dissemination and Follow-Through	– Not messaging work
		– No turn-keying work
	Attitudes and Beliefs	– Dismissing or minimizing the role of race/racism
		– Complaint
		– Denying disproportionality
Midpoint	Overall	– Not a quick fix
		– It will be a journey
		– Building data systems that disaggregate by student social identity markers (e.g., race/ethnicity)
	Logistics	– Commits to the number of training/TA work days
		– Allocates resources for trainings
	Buy-in	– Most participants prepared for session
		– Leaders and other staff begin to champion work
	Dissemination and Follow-Through	– Some messaging about the district's disproportionality has started to occur
		– Data conversations are occurring in the district and schools
	Attitudes and Beliefs	– Realization that the citation is not a quick fix
		– Awareness of district disproportionality
		– Starting to see value of the work

(continued)

Table 7.1. (Continued)

Endpoint	Overall	– Long-term commitment to the work
		– Development of long-term plans
		– Data systems to consistently monitor disproportionality
		– Assign staff/leader to direct the work or creates a position for CRE/equity coordinator
	Logistics	– Commitment to ongoing training
		– Allocation of resources (e.g., time, substitutes for teachers)
		– Scheduling of work ahead of time
	Buy-in	– Identified participants attend the majority of the training/TA sessions
		– District leader and other staff are championing the work
	Dissemination and Follow-Through	– Messaging of work
		– Turn-keying the work
		– Implementing a TTT model
	Attitudes and Beliefs	– Views CRE training as foundation
		– Acknowledging disproportionality
		– Engaging race discussions

Lessons From Our Case Studies

Elmer City School District. The lessons learned from Elmer stressed the potential of creating a districtwide data system to monitor disproportionality that included disaggregation of data by race/ethnicity, gender, IEP/non-IEP status, and multilingual learners. Along with creating the data systems, they also developed a process to distribute disaggregated behavior, attendance, and academic data to building leaders every 6 weeks. Elmer adapted the Guardians of Equity (GoE) protocol (see Chapter 2) and had ongoing, scheduled leadership meetings to engage in data action planning. Subsequent meetings throughout the year were used to monitor the action steps and data.

As such, it is critical that all school-based data is disaggregated by race/ethnicity and IEP status to fully grasp the extent of a district's disproportionality and more importantly, to continually monitor any shifts. In our work with school-based educators, we are often encountered with reasons for a district's inability to take this foundational step. We often hear things like "Our current system doesn't have the ability to do this," or "Our schools all use different systems," or, very often the case, "We were never trained on how to do that." Conversely, in our conversations with district leaders, we frequently were told that their data systems not only have the ability to disaggregate academic and behavioral data, but also that their central office runs those exact reports. This highlights a key tension in the work—the missing link between what is perceived or wishfully thought to be happening in schools by central office with what is actually carried out by school-based administrators and educators. Whether it is a need for a new software platform, the streamlining of existing systems, or more robust training, all districts can and must take this very critical step on their own in order to actively address disproportionate outcomes. Progress monitoring of disaggregated data, particularly if the district has received a state and/or federal notification for disproportionate outcomes, becomes a crucial first step in the change process.

Palisades City School District. In Palisades, we learned that even with the technical tools, the type evidenced in Elmer, transformational leadership and capacity building become essential. Our chapter highlights a distinct need for more research around culturally responsive district leadership in particular. While leadership manuals are a dime a dozen in the field of education, they are largely color-evasive and miss the nuance of the role social identities play in cultivating a culturally responsive learning environment that is modeled by district leaders. At times, district leaders can talk a good game when it comes to issues of equity and disproportionality, but if the self-work isn't happening, the outcomes and experiences of those around them will not radically shift. The superintendent who vocally led equity initiatives in Palisades had many strengths, in tune with the language of equity and systems change, but most critically, was unable to further engage their own racial identity and responsive leadership to build capacity in others in order to effectively shift a culture. This has everything to do with an individual's ability to move past intent and into a focus on impact. How are leaders impacting colleagues in deeper ways than just the application of new equity language? Has leadership modeled personal self-reflection in effort to build it into an institutional practice? (Khalifa, 2018). Are school and district leaders actively connecting self to system to uproot white normative school structures? In the wake of the murder of George Floyd, we have witnessed the book clubs, the equity statements, and the often surface-level work that leans more on "diversity initiatives" than racial justice. The work of eradicating disproportionality for racial equity and justice calls on educators and leaders who demonstrate bravery and courage to take risks and "put something on the line." In an interview about her book *We Want to do*

More Than Survive, Dr. Bettina Love powerfully highlights the needed shift to affect change:

> Allies know all the language, they read all the books, they come to the meeting with all the terms, they read the report before you read the report. I always say allies make Black folks feel bad. . . . They come and they know everything and they good and after the meeting you are like, What we going to do? . . . They [white allies] left already!? . . . That is the difference between an ally and a co-conspirator. . . . Put something on the line for somebody. Take a risk. To see how to use your whiteness. . . . Whiteness is like a bank and the ATM card replenishes itself. So spend it! . . . To be a co-conspirator is to take risks for somebody. Put something on the line. But to use it in a way that you are using your privilege.[1] (Love, 2019)

Palisades offers a cautionary tale of implementation that on paper looks successful and effective in creating systems change. In many ways, there were shifts, but capacity building that inevitably shifts disproportionate outcomes and experiences was hindered by a continued failure to interrogate how whiteness and dynamics of power and privilege impede progress; progress that is only sustained within schools through internal accountability fostered by educators and school leaders; progress that is exemplified by people ready to take a risk and put something on the line.

Hamsburg City School District. The case of Hamsburg further highlighted a readiness challenge, but this time more so with the capacity of CfD associates themselves. Effective disproportionality training and TA support hinges not only on a robust curriculum, as outlined in Chapter 2, but also on the delivery and facilitation of the content and the relationships developed through the ongoing partnership. Over the 15 years as a state TA provider, CfD went through several leadership changes itself. Within these changes came varying levels of support and training for our own associates. If associates are not holding a level of fidelity to an approach that is nuanced and leads with our own understanding of the push necessary to see equity shifts, partnering districts will inevitably experience this gap. When the onboarding process was most successful, new CfD associates shadowed veteran associates/a director for an academic year, with the associate gradually stepping into more content delivery in training and TA sessions. Just as fidelity coaching was provided for partnering co-facilitators, this same level of feedback and practice was critical for associates' personal growth. That said, racial disproportionality training and support comes with a particularly nuanced understanding and lift, as evidenced throughout this book. More than a decorated resume, the right candidate for this work hinges on their ability to engage self, model culturally responsiveness in developing relationships throughout partnering districts, and deeply believing in a pedagogy of opposition. Associates must learn to find comfort in the discomfort.

In Hamsburg, the CfD associates' ability to navigate their own racial identity as it related to the needed in-district work became its own barrier. When white people are tasked with pushing predominately white district leaders to engage in systemic equity shifts, it is critical that there is continuous reflection around how whiteness operates between stakeholders—how, at times, instead of challenging the norm, white people co-sign or fail to intervene or haven't done enough unpacking of their own white racial identity to recognize when they are simply maintaining the status quo. This work extends beyond Hamsburg to any white person tasked with shifting beliefs and systems they inevitably have and still benefit from. The work of recognizing racial identity influence becomes life's work and often, a calling, as our partners in Hayward continued to emphasize.

Hayward Unified School District. Our last case study, in Hayward, exemplified so much of what the everyday, long-term commitment can and should look like. The CRE co-facilitation team in Hayward built in-district capacity with a steadfast determination to immerse themselves in the CfD curriculum and then make it their own. It became work led by district personnel and adjusted based on community expertise. The CRE leaders in Hayward built a system of training and support through internal accountability. Each of them was deeply invested in experiencing a culture change and impacted their varying school and district communities in a way that CfD associates could never do by themselves. Through training multiple cohorts consisting of a diversity of participants (i.e., in district role and social identities), the work started to simultaneously impact BPPPs across the district. We learned that successful training and technical assistance is foundationally people work, relationship building. Hayward in-district co-facilitators shared that through our partnership they felt validated, that sometimes they didn't even realize how hungry they were for a partnership that struggled together to push equity and culturally responsive practices in the district. The leaders in Hayward who took on the task of CRE training are some of the most dedicated educators we have ever met. Traveling to support Hayward didn't feel like a burdensome task, but rather an exciting opportunity to lean in with like-minded educators. The lift felt distributed. It felt like more of a calling, for all of us.

That said, we still witnessed that the incremental shifts can be negatively impacted by leadership change and incoherent messaging. Inconsistent support and investment in the work when superintendent changes occurred left district facilitators with a lot of uphill battles to continue the work. However, through systems buoyed by fully trained and bought-in district employees, the positive ripple effect continues and to this day, has an impact on students, families, and staff. The principal on assignment to run the CRE trainings and support efforts remarked that "it was a blessing to end my career with this work."

In many ways CfD learned alongside district leaders, educators, and community members. In response to many of the in-district challenges and lessons learned, CfD slowly incorporated new approaches to more effectively support partnering districts. Through each partnering district, we continued to look to dismantle disproportionality through directly addressing the belief work, and as state-contracted TA providers tasked with uprooting and shifting systems, we also sought to integrate new frameworks of support to build capacity for actionable steps that would shift district cultures.

Coherence as outlined by Fullan and Quinn (2016) and the parameters offered with implementation science started to become critical conduits to more intentionally attack systemic change, alongside the essential elements of school improvement highlighted in Chapter 2. As the critical self-reflection, part of the adaptive/heart work, is happening within a school system, what is the path forward for implementing a more culturally responsive system? How can we support a school district to be action-driven and *sustain* the everyday work?

STEPS TO SYSTEMIC CHANGE: THE INTERSECTION OF CR-SE, SCHOOL IMPROVEMENT, IMPLEMENTATION SCIENCE, AND COHERENCE

As evident through the case studies in this book, culturally responsive-sustaining education (CR-SE), when merged with the essential elements of school improvement, has the promise of transforming disproportionate outcomes and experiences into sustainable equitable systems. As discussed in Chapter 2, Bryk et al. (2010) offers a school improvement framework, through the lens of five essential supports: (1) Leadership as a Catalyst for Change, (2) Parent and Community Ties, (3) Professional Capacity, (4) Student-Centered Learning Climate, and (5) Instructional Guidance; all of which can lead to significantly decreasing disparate student outcomes (Bryk et al., 2010). For example, the Parent and Community Ties essential support has to be a foundational focus for districts because the building of relational trust is a critical and ongoing process for school communities. Hearts and minds need to be changed in order to truly hold students and families as partners and essential funds of knowledge. Districts approaching families as essential to the schooling process are foundationally doing the work that leads to uprooting a system that continues to marginalize students and families of color. Schools have historically upheld white normative cultural practices and both consciously and unconsciously have required families and students of color to assimilate to these norms (Harry & Klingner, 2014). Building a welcoming and affirming environment starts with being responsive to the school community and challenging the BPPPs that have continually led to disproportionate experiences and outcomes.

Figure 7.1. Intersecting Frameworks

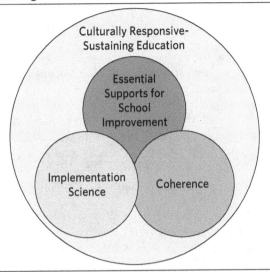

Culturally responsive-sustaining education continues to be the foundation for the needed systemic change in schools. To effectively implement this change, as pictured in Figure 7.1, our work has leaned on the intersection of the following frameworks: Essential Supports for School Improvement (Bryk et al., 2010), Implementation Science (Jackson et al., 2018), and Coherence (Fullan & Quinn, 2016).

Essential Supports for School Improvement

When school leaders and practitioners create welcoming and affirming spaces to engage with families—particularly families of racial/ethnic and cultural difference—the more likely they are to build deeper relationships. Educators with deeper student and family ties become less likely to make a choice to negligently suspend and/or unnecessarily recommend a student for special education placement, but rather lean into a relationship and community-based approach first and foremost.

Implementation Science

Districts must start systemic work by coming up with culturally responsive usable practices and aligned implementation drivers (strategies) that are buoyed by improvement cycles (periodic review of progress) (Jackson et al., 2018) to shift the current disproportionate racialized classification, discipline, and academic outcomes. The usable practices are the overarching CR-SE goals that will lead to change. The chosen usable practice should directly connect to the desired outcome goals a district may have. For example, a district may recognize through the root cause process that they lack a data system to effectively track and respond to existing disproportionality, so they develop the following usable practice to live in their strategic plan:

> *Develop and use a sustainable data system that informs instruction and decision-making to address the disproportionate outcomes of students who are historically marginalized.*

The change drivers are the strategies that will be implemented to accomplish the expressed usable practice. These strategies can be based on building further competency, organizational capacity, and/or leadership ability in the district. They become the methods to accomplishing the goal embedded in the usable practice. For the example above, one of the drivers becomes:

> *Identify current data being collected in each school in the district and how it is/is not disaggregated (e.g., race/ethnicity, IEP status). Create a document highlighting what is happening at each school in the district and the needs based on this review.*

In creating a multi-year, strategic action plan, a district may have three to five focus areas (e.g., data systems, restorative practices, multi-tiered system of support, professional development and support, teaching and learning) that each have an overarching usable practice (that doesn't change over the multiple years), implementation drivers and teams, along with outlined improvement cycles to monitor and review progress. Implementation teams are identified for each of the focus areas.

> *What employees in the district have the experience in each focus area and have the reach to message and implement the work moving forward?*

Teams also identify what phase of implementation they are in for each focus area. In accordance with implementation science, districts should think about systemic shifts in 1–5-year phases. Phase 1 designated as *Exploration,* is where research and review become critical to assess and create readiness. With the example above, this could mean reaching out to other districts that already have data systems similar to what the district wants to implement. Phase 2 is about *Installation* and bringing together the appropriate resources (personnel and financial) to ensure successful implementation. This includes training district and school staff on the data systems. Phase 3 starts the *Initial Implementation* where districts lean into the use of the practice; in this case, a new data system that is monitoring and supporting ongoing review of district disproportionality. Finally, Phase 4 is *Full Implementation* and ideally occurs within 2–4 years of the writing of the district's strategic plan. For this example, a district will have fully trained staff on the data system and action planning protocols, and an embedded culture of disaggregated data and review that leads seamlessly to ongoing action to disrupt and dismantle the disproportionate student outcomes that surface. Finally, while teams are moving through the academic year, taking direction from their usable practice and implementation drivers, improvement cycles guide the ongoing process. Also known as PDSA cycles, these become the mechanism for monitoring change. Often occurring in 6–8-week increments, teams come together to: (1) Plan—identify the current next steps, (2) Do—carry them out with a clear timeline and understanding, (3) Study—discuss what the results were, and (4) Act—address any changes that need to be made based on the findings.

All of these steps must be grounded in CR-SE. It is critical that districts develop race-conscious, precise goals and clearly identify "the who" in regard to who will benefit from the outlined plan. This level of strategic planning has to be driven by an equity lens that engages a sociopolitical, historical view of the district's community. *Who has been and is currently impacted negatively by the system? How is this plan going to directly provide more equity for the given group(s)? How will the district hold itself accountable to taking these active, everyday steps in carrying out the plan outlined?*

Coherence

We know that the success of a district's strategic plan has everything to do with how the work is messaged and who is involved in the creation and messaging process. A coherence framework focuses purpose and clarity on work that aims to impact student learning and outcomes. Coherence consists of the shared depth of understanding about the purpose and nature of work. What is in the minds and actions of people individually and collectively? To that end, the coherence framework builds on focusing direction, cultivating collaborative cultures, deepening learning, and securing accountability (Fullan & Quinn, 2016). "Focusing direction" is about integrating the scope of work into the existing system. To fully execute the focused direction, districts must cultivate collaborative cultures to support individuals and grow groups who will be able to execute the work. Deepening learning is fundamental among collaborative cultures to shape better outcomes. All of this work takes time along with a marked intention and investment. We have witnessed far too many efforts fall short because of a lack of coherence in messaging, collaboration, and accountability.

THEORY OF CHANGE—CONNECTING A CULTURALLY RESPONSIVE SELF TO A CULTURALLY RESPONSIVE SYSTEM

The essential supports for school improvement, implementation science, and coherence fall flat if CR-SE is not the plate—the foundation from which all other pieces are built. After CfD's 15-year partnership with the state came to a close in 2018, the authors of this book continued the work through a new subunit called Center for Systemic Change (CSC). CSC became a natural extension of CfD, building on the legacy of so many

Figure 7.2. CSC Theory of Change

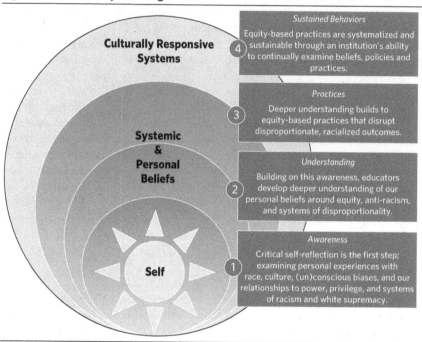

Sustained Behaviors
Equity-based practices are systematized and sustainable through an institution's ability to continually examine beliefs, policies and practices.

Practices
Deeper understanding builds to equity-based practices that disrupt disproportionate, racialized outcomes.

Understanding
Building on this awareness, educators develop deeper understanding of our personal beliefs around equity, anti-racism, and systems of disproportionality.

Awareness
Critical self-reflection is the first step; examining personal experiences with race, culture, (un)conscious biases, and our relationships to power, privilege, and systems of racism and white supremacy.

Culturally Responsive Systems

Systemic & Personal Beliefs

Self

associates and directors that had come before. The expanded iteration of training and TA focuses on educators' and leaders' beliefs around self and systems. These beliefs must be addressed before sustainability of practices and systems can occur. Figure 7.2 and the description of each step that follows outlines the ongoing CR-SE journey that individuals and districts need to commit to—this is the work.

Everything starts with building awareness. This first step to becoming a culturally responsive educator—and eventually a culturally responsive system—hinges on an individual's ability to examine personal identities and relationships to power, privilege, and systems of racism and white supremacy. This is self-work; a focus on individual narratives and ways of being in order to build personal capacity to critically self-reflect. This process heightens awareness of systems of inequality that exist and personal connections one might have to these systems.

From awareness builds deeper understanding. Awareness itself calls into question how systems may or may not be operating. Understanding develops the capacity to engage. By understanding personal impact and where systems of disproportionality and inequity live, individuals are able to connect the personal to what is systemic and in doing so, grow a readiness to shift systems. In schools, educators start asking questions like, "How might my own responses to behavior in my classroom play into a behavioral system that disproportionately impacts Black, Indigenous, and Latinx students in particular?" "What changes do I need to make in how I build relationships across racial and cultural difference in effort to develop a more welcoming and affirming space?"

The reflections that are built from a heightened awareness and understanding inevitably impact and shift practices. White, normative structures of schooling are challenged.

Cultural responsiveness becomes a foundation, the plate, to which all practices must sit. Educators think not only about shifting their pedagogical practices, but also about the needs for more responsive curricula. Everyday actions connect to school- and district-level policies and procedures.

School-based practices start to develop sustained behaviors—behaviors that become part of the central DNA of a school system. At this point, individual learning has moved into group learning, and group learning has developed internal capacity where in-district personnel begin to lead the work. It becomes sustained within the system, not as an add on, but as a foundation to learning and teaching.

CSC holds that the learning process is never static, never linear, and always nuanced. It is important to continually highlight and connect to the historic and sociopolitical context of schooling throughout the change process. To that end, it is also critical to weave identity self-reflection throughout, building a system that continually monitors progress through reflection and data analysis. Self-work and systems work become bedrock to developing and sustaining a culturally responsive environment.

WHEN THE RUBBER MEETS THE ROAD . . .

For years, the authors of this book have all been immersed in the training and technical assistance process, pushing dozens of districts throughout the state and country to take an actively antiracist, culturally responsive approach to disrupting and dismantling the disproportionate outcomes and experiences in our communities. We have continued to urge districts to look at their data and listen to students and caregivers, particularly those who have always been pushed to the margins. We have called on district leaders to center the voices of the most marginalized and make this the entry point to the critical work of unlearning and re-imagining. This looks like ensuring that district and school teams and committees have student and family voices of color represented and that leadership decisions are actively guided by these experiences and expertise. It also looks like cultivating safe spaces for Black student unions and similar student groups who are still most negatively impacted by the culture in so many of our schools. We must hold space for these voices, listen to them, and for many of us, engage what it means to be a co-conspirator (Love, 2019) in the struggle for equity and justice in our schools. If we start there, *every* student will benefit.

Since the beginning of 2020, race-conscious work in schools has been met with a noticeably heightened, vitriolic pushback. Sparked by protests pitting Critical Race Theory (CRT) as the evil infiltrating the minds of our students and teachers across the country, a new wave of attempts (with some success) at banning curriculum, lessons, and professional development about race/racism has surfaced (Pollock & Rogers, 2022). In their report, Pollock and Rogers (2022) found that at least 35% of all K–12 students in the United States have been impacted by the anti "CRT"[2] efforts. Personally, we have experienced several superintendents and school leaders balking under this pressure. We have had anti "CRT" groups Zoom bomb, record, and heckle during our own training sessions. That said, we have also witnessed young folks, particularly Black students, in each of these district spaces continue to organize and demand schools respond to the inequities that exist, to the anti-Black racism that is still pervasive and to the racial gaslighting that continues to impede progress.

Engaging in our own process of reflection by way of this book journey has worked to strengthen our resolve in the work ahead. It is clear to us that the only way forward sits with a forged effort to be race-conscious and to understand how social identity, power, and privilege continually shape experiences in classroom spaces and maintain systemic oppression. It is clear to us that we need to attack disproportionality as a general education issue—to fix the foundational cracks in our system in order to support the inequitable outcomes we continue to see in spaces like special education. It is clear to us that true growth also lives with honoring the experiences of communities that have been and continue to be harmed and not invalidating these realities with misguided attempts at moving forward without connecting the past to the present. We deeply believe that this work has to be a continual process of engaging self and systems, the adaptive and the technical, interrogating beliefs in order to co-create a better, more justice-driven future for our students and ourselves.

Key Interventions for Addressing Disproportionality

Essential Support (Adapted from Bryk et al., 2010)	Key Interventions for Addressing Disproportionality (Adapted from Harry & Klingner, 2014)
Leadership as a driver of change	❑ Conduct a root cause analysis rooted in equity and culture responsiveness ❑ Establish protocols for effective implementation of federal and state policy at the school level ❑ Adapt all systems to value culture, language, heritage, and experiences of diverse students ❑ Establish a data-driven culture and evidence-based instruction, establish mechanisms for teacher support, and development ❑ Establish distributed leadership protocols ❑ Establish decision-making processes that are equity based ❑ Re-examine resource allocation, hire and place qualified practitioners ❑ Establish equitable distribution of quality instruction schoolwide
Build Professional Staff Capacity	❑ Train everyone in Culturally Responsive Education and focus on student assets ❑ Provide pre-service and in-service training ❑ Provide continuous professional development ❑ Establish annual professional development plan and schedule
Establish Instructional Guidance System	❑ Align beliefs, policies, and practices; and all programs ❑ Establish school instructional support systems and adapt interventions, such as RTI, PBIS, classroom management, and other alternative to suspensions ❑ Establish pre-referral interventions ❑ Establish protocols for classroom observations prior to referral

(continued)

Essential Support (Adapted from Bryk et al., 2010)	Key Interventions for Addressing Disproportionality (Adapted from Harry & Klingner, 2014)
Student-Centered Learning Climate	❑ Establish Culturally Responsive assessment techniques schoolwide ❑ Increase academic language proficiency and develop Culturally Responsive Curriculum ❑ Provide early intervening services and quality early childhood ❑ Decrease class size for struggling students in resource, pull out, and self-contained ❑ Establish inclusive classrooms and social emotional programs
Family and Community ties	❑ Involve all families and community in assessment, placement, and policy-making decisions

Example Survey Questions

Culturally Responsive Instruction

I am knowledgeable about the history and cultures of diverse ethnic, racial, and cultural groups.

I am knowledgeable about my students' individual learning styles.

I am able to modify my instruction so that students from diverse ethnic, racial, cultural, language, and ability groups will have an equal opportunity to learn.

It is not so important to utilize instructional materials that reflect images and perspectives from diverse groups.

Self-Efficacy

If students aren't disciplined at home, they aren't likely to accept any discipline.

When a student gets a better grade than they usually gets, it is usually because I found better ways of teaching that student.

Teachers are not a very powerful influence on student achievement when all factors are considered.

If a student in my class becomes disruptive and noisy, I feel assured that I know some techniques to redirect them quickly.

Perspective on Early Intervention

If I feel that a student is struggling in my class, I know where to access resources in the school that will help me teach that student more effectively.

My school has an effective pre-referral/early intervention process to meet the academic needs of struggling learners.

If I feel that a student is exhibiting behavior problems in my class, I know where to access resources in the school that will help me manage that student's behavior more effectively.

Referral Process

When a student is exhibiting an academic and/or behavioral difficulty, I can refer them to my school's pre-referral or early intervention system.

Over the past YEAR, how many referrals to your school's pre-referral or early interventions system did you make?

Over the past YEAR, how many students did you refer to your school's pre-referral or early interventions system?

(continued)

Perspectives on Culture and Race

Thinking or talking about race makes me feel uncomfortable.

Sometimes I wonder why we can't see each other as individuals instead of race always being an issue.

The values and beliefs shared by those in disadvantaged neighborhoods tend to go against school values and beliefs about what makes up a good education.

Students of color from disadvantaged homes just seem to show a lack of initiative.

Example Belief, Policy, and Practice Root Cause Table

Root Cause	Beliefs	Policies	Practices
Discipline Policies and Practices	*Disruptive students should be removed *Some students do not value education *Consequences are needed for behaviors/Punitive consequences are effective *Hooded sweatshirts, bandanas and hats can be associated with problematic behavior and criminal activity	*Zero tolerance *Code of Conduct	*Relying on removal of students/classroom managed behaviors are passed off to the administration *Restorative practices are partially in place/inconsistent *Code of conduct inconsistently followed, implemented, or applied *Teachers, staff, and administration escalate student behavior *Very subjective reasons for discipline and referrals
Interventions and Referrals	*Teachers aren't aware of interventions *Means more work *"These kids can't do it" *A punishment is an intervention *Students who put their head down, are noisy, not doing work should be referred to SST *SPED will solve the problem	*School Support Teams (SST) *Tiered interventions PBIS *Unclear policy on academic referral aside from CSE	*African American students and students with an IEP are referred at a higher rate *Instruction is not culturally responsiveness *Lack of collection of data *Lack of consistency in interventions *Too quick to refer to special education

Instruction and Assessment	*All students learn the same *Teacher feels like kids cannot achieve	*Implement a strict curriculum and pacing guide *Standardized testing	*Lack of differentiation and scaffolding *District plans/curriculum delivery varies *We lower rigor *Data does not always drive instruction *Continue to follow same practices, expecting different results
Educational Opportunity	*Students would not take advantage of opportunity if given *Only some can reach high standards *Students unprepared from earlier grades *Deficit thinking of students	*Criteria based schools *Community school	*Not all schools have same resources/budgets are not equitable *Some students receive different opportunities *No AP/IB courses in all schools *Not enough courses relevant to students
Family and Community	*Poverty; no desire to improve; "don't value education." *All kids are poor in urban setting *Disability in many homes Home environment—parents need to do more for their children *Too many young parents	*Family Engagement policy *Community schools	*Only negative calls home *Building level attempts to engage parents/caregivers varies *Lack of communication with parents/caregivers *Engage with parents/caregivers who are already engaged *No support from district in getting parents involved Certain parents/caregivers are not well received

(continued)

Root Cause	Beliefs	Policies	Practices
Educators' Expectations and Misconceptions	*Low expectations for low achieving students; home life *Low expectations/bias against certain groups *"They can't read" *"They don't want to learn"	*Lowered passing grade from 75 to 65	*Inflexible curriculum pacing and expectations of students *Color-evasiveness *Academic assignments lack rigor *Students "just should know" expectations
Cultural Dissonance	*There are too many cultures to address all *Color-evasiveness and culture don't matter and are not related to the classroom *White culture is to be aspired *Students need to assimilate quickly *Students need to do it "my way" *It's not my job to teach students about their culture	*None	*Lack of cultural awareness *Lack of culturally relevant teaching *Multicultural night *Lack of training for staff *Lack of diverse staff
Socio-Demographics	*Teachers overgeneralize about who students are *Biased based on race, class, gender *Low SES leads to lower performance *Poor underprivileged dysfunctional homes with low education families	*School of choice	*Over referral for discipline issues and to special education *"Savior" mentality devalues culture/experiences resiliency *Segregated schools

Application Scenario Examples

SCENARIO 1

You overhear Ms. Stewart, a white teacher, talking to Mr. Ryan, a Black teacher, in the faculty lounge about Sherry, a Black student. Ms. Stewart says the following: "She would do so much better if she knew how to behave. But she probably doesn't have a good situation at home. Her mother works a lot and she is not home to care for her, and she doesn't care about her children's education. I feel so bad for her, she is failing. I will keep on writing her up if this behavior continues. If she can't make it to my class, she may need to go to a 15:1." Mr. Ryan responds: "I have a lot of those kinds of students too whose parents don't care about their education, and aren't going to make it in my class."

Questions:

1. What would you do?
2. Develop a written script on how you would address the interaction between Ms. Stewart and Mr. Ryan.
3. Role play your script.

What to consider:

1. Who is mostly adversely affected by this issue? Who faces racial barriers or bias, or exclusion from power related to this situation?
2. How are individuals of different racial groups differently situated or affected?
3. What role does your race/ethnicity, gender, current SES, etc. play in this situation?
4. How do race, power, privilege, fairness, access, opportunity, and equity intersect in this situation?
5. What do you have to consider about your social identity and social positioning that may impact the way you respond in this situation?

Reflection:

1. How does your equity lens guide how you approached the situation?
2. What overt beliefs, policies, procedures, or practices guided how you approached the situation?
3. What covert (hidden) beliefs, policies, procedures, or practices guided how you approached the situation?

SCENARIO 2

You are sitting in on a CSE meeting of Don, a Black boy who has been absent a lot. The CSE committee is waiting for Don's parent to arrive. His classroom teacher Ms. Hardy (who is White) says: "She probably isn't coming, she never comes to school." Mrs. Bryan, Don's mom, comes in with two of her younger children. Mrs. Bryan is wearing a winter cap, a sweatshirt and sweat pants, and smells like cigarettes. Ms. Hardy shares the following: "Don is failing the class and needs to be in Special Education. He does not have the pre-requisite skills to succeed in a 6th-grade math class, and his reading comprehension is lacking, impeding his ability to grasp new concepts. He is also a poor writer. The class size might be too big for him because he cannot concentrate." When Mrs. Bryan leaves, Ms. Hardy says: "No wonder Don can't concentrate, did you smell her?"

Questions:

1. What would you do?
2. Develop a written script on how you would address the comments made during the CSE meeting and by Ms. Hardy.
3. Role play your script.

What to consider:

1. Who is mostly adversely affected by this issue? Who faces racial barriers or bias, or exclusion from power related to this situation?
2. How are individuals of different racial groups differently situated or affected?
3. What role does your race/ethnicity, gender, current SES, etc. play in this situation?
4. How do race, power, privilege, fairness, access, opportunity, and equity intersect in this situation?
5. What do you have to consider about your social identity and social positioning that may impact the way you respond in this situation?

Reflection:

1. How does your equity lens guide how you approached the situation?
2. What overt beliefs, policies, procedures, or practices guided how you approached the situation?
3. What covert (hidden) beliefs, policies, procedures, or practices guided how you approached the situation?

District Leadership Example Priorities and Goal Example

Priority: Addressing Racial Injustices	
Goal	**Implementation Strategy**
Address Racial Injustice at the District Level	Create equitable (not equal) allocations of Staff and Resources: Needs-based budgeting and allocations
	Create board policies to proactively confront racialized outcomes specific to: a) Access to advanced coursework b) Grading practices c) Student Enrollment/Assignment: proportional access to programs, school choice, and neighborhood schools
	Review Curriculum, Teaching Practices, Training modules, and Resources for alignment with culturally responsive pedagogy (CRE Audit)
Address Racial Injustice at the School Level	Incorporate CRE training into School-Based Professional Learning: PLCs
	Host student leadership forums to gather student input on experienced injustices and strategies for confronting stated injustices

Priority: Transparency Around Outcomes for Historically Marginalized Students	
Goal	**Implementation Strategy**
To create Data Dashboard	Decide which sets of data will be collected
	Review existing Data Dashboards, and equity report cards to advise on most efficient format and content
To create District Equity Report Card	Decide which "outcomes" will be reported
	Establish procedures for collecting data
	Create a "marketing" plan for disseminating data

(continued)

Priority: Human resources—recruit, hire, develop, support, and retain the most effective staff that closely mirrors the student in the district.

Goal	Implementation Strategy
Recruit and Retain	Survey staff of color in order to determine the challenges we face with recruitment/retention
	Review disaggregated data to set baselines for recruitment/ retention of staff
Hire	Create a pipeline and grow our own diverse staff
Support	Build out networking opportunities for building supportive relationships among diverse staff
	Provide PD on CRE for peer observances and other HR staff

Strategic Action Plan Example Strategies

Priority	Strategy	Strategy
Engage Families and Communities	Every division and school will develop written plans that define action steps with customized targets for increasing engagement of their families.	All schools will conduct quarterly data (academic, behavioral, attendance) review sessions with families using district-aligned resources (e.g., PEN PALS).
Implement Culturally Responsive Practices	Complete a curriculum, district policy and practice audit for cultural relevance and implement corrective actions.	All staff will have received standardized, baseline Culturally Responsive Education (CRE) professional development from which schools and staff can personalize their support.
Recruit, Develop, Support and Retain the Most Effective Diverse Staff	Educate all employees on our district's core values, culture and high expectations, and measure efficacy of the effort based on surveys.	Provide and expand professional learning opportunities for all employee groups in leadership development and other job-related training.
Personalize Learning for Students	The district will have a common understanding and corresponding approach to personalized learning.	100% of teachers will leverage personalized learning strategies that will help students achieve their goals.

(*continued*)

Priority	Strategy	Strategy
Provide Dynamic, Rigorous Curriculum and Instruction	Develop action plans for leveraging all content areas. All content areas will develop common benchmark assessments for all grades.	Implement and use data from common benchmarks for all content areas across grade levels.

CfD Readiness Tool

CFD DISTRICT READINESS EXPLORATION TOOL

The CfD District Readiness Exploration Tool will be utilized prior to root cause during work with a district. It will be completed by CfD in collaboration with school district leaders to determine the level of readiness to address disproportionality. Complete the readiness tool based on your respective role in the district. A 0–4 Likert scale ranging from never to all the time will be used and a composite score will be calculated to assess a district's readiness. The scores will be aligned with the level of readiness criterion noted on the CfD Readiness Scale following the tool. The result will be a snapshot indication of the district's readiness to begin addressing issues related to disproportionality.

	Level of Readiness				
	Never (0)	Once in a while (1)	Some of the time (2)	Very often (3)	All the time (4)
School district leaders recognize disproportionality exists and acknowledge the citation.					
School district leaders[1] (i.e., superintendents, central office district administrators and school building principals and identified teacher leaders) recognize that disproportionality occurs within the district and are implementing initiatives (e.g., assessed their policies and practices) to begin to address disproportionality.					

(continued)

	Level of Readiness				
	Never (0)	Once in a while (1)	Some of the time (2)	Very often (3)	All the time (4)
A policy for disaggregating discipline and academic achievement data by race and ethnicity exists and a team exists that analyzes this data.					
A district team exists that analyzes disaggregated discipline and academic achievement data by race and ethnicity.					
A policy for addressing disproportionality exists.					
District leaders expect that stakeholders (e.g., building leaders, teacher leaders, teachers, etc.) address disproportionality.					
The school district is able to have difficult conversations about race and ethnicity and disproportionate student outcomes.					
District leaders are able to articulate disparities by race and ethnicity.					
There is buy-in from the school district about disproportionality, including district leaders publicly acknowledge the citation (on the website, at a school board meeting).					
District leaders engage openly in conversations around disproportionate outcomes.					
District leaders engage openly in conversations around addressing disproportionality.					
District leaders engage openly in conversations around race, ethnicity, and language differences and culturally responsive practices.					

(continued)

	Level of Readiness				
	Never (0)	Once in a while (1)	Some of the time (2)	Very often (3)	All the time (4)
An infrastructure exists in the district to address disproportionality. School district systems that exist to address disproportionality are implemented with fidelity.					
School district leaders have developed a structure to address disproportionate outcomes.					
District leaders share a vision for equity with school community members.					
The equity vision is evident, not only on the website and other documentation, but in leader's policy and practice decisions.					
The district vision supports the implementation and development of culturally responsive practices.					
District leaders monitor and evaluate how well instructional support systems are working to support equity.					
District leaders monitor and evaluate how well discipline support systems are working to support equity.					
District leaders monitor and evaluate how well academic support systems are working to support equity.					
District hiring practices thoughtfully result in a staff that represents the student and community population.					
School district relationships with stakeholders (e.g., building leaders, teacher leaders, teachers, families, students, community etc.) are transformational.					
District leaders have a mission and vision for the district.					

(continued)

	Level of Readiness				
	Never (0)	Once in a while (1)	Some of the time (2)	Very often (3)	All the time (4)
This mission and vision are communicated in all interactions and district improvement plans.					
District leaders are critical and reflective on policies and practices and the impact of each on student outcomes.					

School district leaders build systems within each of the other essential supports (professional staff capacity, instructional guidance, student-centered learning climate, and family/community partnerships) to address disproportionate outcomes.

School district leaders ensure **professional staff capacity** to address disproportionate outcomes.					
Staff is trained in implementing culturally responsive instructional practices.					
Professional development and coaching are offered to support culturally responsive practices.					
Problem-solving teams actively analyze discipline and academic achievement data disaggregated by race, ethnicity, gender, IEP, and ENL.					
School district leaders ensure the **instructional guidance** system is culturally responsive, including materials and curriculum that represent the student and community population.					
School district leaders foster a positive **student-centered learning climate,** including leaders who have a clear vision for student and staff culture.					
There is a collegial and positive tone in staff interactions.					
The staff morale is high and burnout is low in the district.					
Students are supported academically.					

(continued)

	Level of Readiness				
	Never (0)	Once in a while (1)	Some of the time (2)	Very often (3)	All the time (4)
Students are given clear behavioral expectations.					
School district leaders prioritize **family and community** members as partners in learning.					
District leaders access the varied perspectives of all school community members.					
District leaders make changes to policies based on the varied perspectives of all school community members.					
District leaders make changes to practices based on the varied perspectives of all school community members.					
TOTAL					

The scores from the CfD District Readiness Exploration Tool will be aligned with the level of readiness criterion noted below.

District Level	Notes
1. *No Awareness*: School district does not believe that they have a problem with disproportionality, and perceive inappropriate classifications and suspensions for certain student groups as part of common practices.	
2. *Denial*: School district acknowledges some disproportionality exist within district, but only focus on isolated, such as AIS, with very little attention more systemic issues or perceive that because of poverty they cannot reduce disproportionality.	
3. *Vague awareness*: School district recognizes that disproportionality occurs within the district and want to do something but are uncertain on how to begin to best address disproportionality.	
4. *Awareness:* School district recognizes that disproportionality occurs within the district and have started working on initiatives (e.g., assessed their policies and practices) to begin to address disproportionality.	

Glossary

Term	Definition
Educational Equity	"To be achieved and sustained, equity needs to be thought of as a structural and systemic concept, and not as idealistic. Equity is a robust system and dynamic process that reinforces and replicates equitable ideas, power, resources, strategies, conditions, habits, and outcomes. The state, quality, or ideal of being just, impartial, and fair. The concept of equity is synonymous with fairness and justice." (NYSED, 2019)
	"Educational equity incorporates educational policies, practices, interactions, and resources that are representative of, constructed by, and responsive to every student such that each individual has access to and can meaningfully participate and make progress in high-quality learning experiences that support students toward self-determination and reduce disparities in outcomes regardless of individual differences and social identities." (Great Lakes Equity Center, 2013; Fraser, 2008).
Educational Equality	Educational equality is the principle of allocating educational resources with an emphasis on the equal distribution of inputs without attention given to the corresponding outputs.
Disproportionality	The over-representation of a specific group in special education programs or disciplinary outcomes relative to the presence of this group in the overall student population, and/or the underrepresentation of a specific group in accessing intervention services, resources, programs, rigorous curriculum and instruction relative to the presence of this group in the overall student population.
	The outcome of institutionalized racism and bias that result in discriminatory beliefs, policies, and practices, which negatively affect historically marginalized groups in contrast to privileged groups.

(continued)

Term	Definition
IDEA	"The Individuals with Disabilities Education Act (IDEA) is a law that makes available a free appropriate public education to eligible children with disabilities throughout the nation and ensures special education and related services to children who qualify.
	The IDEA governs how states and public agencies provide early intervention, special education, and related services to more than 7.5 million (as of school year 2018–19) eligible infants, toddlers, children, and youth with disabilities."
	IDEA introduced the monitoring of disproportionality in 1997 and in 2004, it included the provision to disaggregate by race. This included requiring State Education Agencies (SEAs) to prioritize monitoring the outcomes of classification patterns, classification categories, placements of students, and suspension of students with an IEP by race/ethnicity. That said, as a policy, IDEA has been largely race-neutral because states and districts have not effectively addressed the root causes of racial disproportionality.
Composition Index	Composition index gives the proportion of students by race/ethnicity in a particular outcome. Composition indexes are used to determine if a particular group is over or underrepresented in a particular outcome. For example, Latinx students make up 25% of a school population, but receive 50% of all suspensions in a given year.
Risk Index	Risk index is the representation of a racial/ethnic group in a particular outcome in comparison to total enrollment of that specific racial/ethnic group. For example, 30 Black students are involved in the disciplinary outcome out of a total 100 Black students enrolled. The risk Index for Black students stands at 30%. In other words, Black students are at a 30% risk of being represented in a disciplinary action.
Relative Risk Ratio	Relative risk ratio, also referred to as "relative risk," is the risk of one racial/ethnic group in comparison to the risk of all other racial/ethnic groups to experience an outcome. A risk ratio of 1 indicates a racial/ethnic group has equal risk in comparison to all other groups for a particular outcome; less than 1 means underrepresentation of a racial/ethnic group; and higher than 1 means a racial/ethnic group is at an elevated risk in comparison to the other racial/ethnic groups. For example, if 50 out of 100

(*continued*)

Term	Definition
	Black students were suspended, creating a risk of 50%, whereas only 50 out of 200 students from all other racial/ethnic groups were suspended creating a risk of 25%, the relative risk ratio for Black students is 2, which means Black students are 2 times more likely to be suspended as compared to all other students. The relative risk ratio is often a preferred method of calculation because it offers a comparative index of risk (Klingner et al., 2005).
Deficit Thinking	The act or process of placing the blame of achievement and opportunity gaps on students, families, and their communities. It pathologizes groups and discounts the role of educational systems in manufacturing and maintaining racial inequities. Much of the foundation of deficit thinking is based on fallacious genetic deficits and the myth of a culture of poverty (Valencia, 1997).
Poverty Disciplining	The act or process of punishing the behaviors and thinking held by people from low-income backgrounds. Poverty disciplining moves to change the behavior of these individuals to reflect that of the white middle class. It is important to note that while this belief does not explicitly focus on race it is often used as a proxy to blame Black and other people of color for the conditions of schooling and their academic achievement (Fergus, 2017, 2019).
Color-evasive	A dominant belief that purports seeing and talking about race as problematic. Individuals that hold a color-evasive lens contend that "seeing everyone the same" is actually the most fair way to engage difference. However, the impact of such a belief discredits and denies the role that racism plays in the lived experiences of various racial groups and obscures its role in systemic inequities. Additionally, we are often left with blaming the individuals and communities for the impact of systemic racism when we maintain a color-evasive lens (Bonilla-Silva, 2003).
Culturally Responsive-Sustaining Education (CR-SE)	Education that is grounded in a cultural view of learning and human development in which multiple expressions of diversity (e.g., race, social class, gender, language, sexual orientation, nationality, religion, ability) are recognized as assets for teaching and learning." There are four principles critical in developing a CR-S environment: (1) *Welcoming and Affirming Environment*, (2) *High Expectations and Rigorous Instruction*, (3) *Inclusive Curriculum and Assessment*, and (4) *Ongoing Professional Learning* (NYSED, 2019).

(continued)

Term	Definition
Professional Development/ Learning	The ongoing learning that is offered to educators within a school and/or district. Professional development in schools requires an investment of time and often monetary resources and becomes vital for educators and school/ district leaders to continue to grow and effectively support first and foremost, every child, but also family and community members.
Technical Assistance (TA) in Education	The process of providing targeted support to a school and/ or district in an effort to build capacity to solve problems that may exist and/or develop new competencies that are used to better serve school-based stakeholders (e.g., teachers, students, families). Ideal TA builds the internal capacity of the recipient to ultimately shift systems.
White Privilege	A built-in advantage, for white people, separate from one's level of income or effort based on a sociopolitical, historical grounding that white is ideal and normative. It also lives as a subconscious preference perpetuated by white people's lack of awareness that they hold this power. White privilege is both unconsciously enjoyed and consciously perpetuated (Learning for Justice, 2018).
Systemic Racism	Racism is the use of race to establish and justify a social hierarchy and system of power that privileges, preferences or advances certain individuals or groups of people (white people), usually at the expense of others. Systemic racism occurs and is maintained through structures like schools, businesses and governments as they exert power and privilege that expressly benefit white people while continuing to marginalize people of color (Tatum, 2003).
Whiteness	Whiteness operates within a system of racism and actively elevates white people over people of color. This concept counters how racism is consistently believed to exist in education, as specific, abhorrent actions by individuals (e.g., hate speech, actions of overtly white supremacist groups). Whiteness also goes beyond just naming *white privileges*.
	Whiteness operates at all times within institutions such as schooling and directly impacts beliefs, policies, practices, and procedures. Whiteness in schools manifests through claiming that certain values and experiences are shared by all when they are actually only afforded to white people.

(*continued*)

Term	Definition
Marginalized	Refers to the unequal treatment and active maintenance of the oppression of individuals and groups. Often referred to as "historically marginalized," in the context of this book the authors highlight that marginalizations experienced in schools are historic and also current.
Intersectionality/ Intersectional Analysis	Intersectionality, as coined by Kimberlé Crenshaw, "is a lens, a prism, for seeing the way in which various forms of inequality often operate together and exacerbate each other."
	An intersectional analysis, as it relates to disproportionality work in education, looks at student experience and outcome data from multiple perspectives, disaggregating the data by various social identity markers (e.g., race/ethnicity, SES, gender-identity, IEP status) to more fully understand where inequities are present (Crenshaw, 1991).
Race-Based Bias/ Prejudice	For prejudice:
	A prejudgment or unjustifiable, and usually negative, attitude of one type of individual or groups toward another group and its members. Such negative attitudes are typically based on unsupported generalizations (or stereotypes) that deny the right of individual members of certain groups to be recognized and treated as individuals with individual characteristics (Tatum, 2003).

Notes

Chapter 1

1. All names of schools, districts, or their personnel are pseudonyms to protect the privacy of our partners. In addition, we aim to remove any other identifying information from this book.

2. We use Latinx to offer a gender-neutral identifier for Latino/a.

3. We refer to the State Department of Education in which our work is situated as the State.

4. Toward the end of the CfD's contract, associates often utilized opening and closing circles, drawing from restorative practices, where learners connect through sharing in a circle formation, using prompts and specific sharing procedures.

5. We identify marginalized communities as being historically AND presently marginalized and will operate with this understanding when we use "marginalized" throughout this book.

6. Throughout much of CfD's work we referred to CR-SE as Culturally Responsive Education (CRE) and later moved to incorporate Sustaining based on the contributions of Dr. Django Paris and Dr. H. Sammy Alim.

7. Many people have referred to this belief as being "colorblind." However, we believe this language to be ableist in nature as it refers to an actual diagnosis and move to maintain the concept but reframe from ableist language. In addition, color-evasiveness signifies that this belief is active.

8. While CRE urges us to take a broader look at the impact of race, ethnicity, and culture for every student and particularly for students of color who have been historically and currently marginalized, we primarily focus on Black and Latinx students in this book because most of the citations live with these students in the particular state. Moreover, when we only mention Black or Latinx students it is because we believe being more specific is warranted. We acknowledge that Latinx students can also be Black.

Chapter 2

1. When we mention vulnerability, we mean students and families that are vulnerable to experiencing racism and race-based prejudice.

2. Session titles and content shifted over the 15-year period of CfD. These descriptions come from the most recent iteration of the curriculum, 2014–2019.

3. CfD slide 21, Session 1, research source: Annie E. Casey Foundation, Race Matters.

Chapter 3

1. An Assurance of Discontinuance is an alternative to administrative or judicial proceedings that lay out specific actions that must be taken to address a violation of law.

Chapter 4

1. Early warning systems are systems that use student data to identify students who exhibit behavior or academic performance delays that puts them "at risk" of dropping out of school (U.S. Department of Education, 2016).

2. The relative risk ratio provides a comparison of one racial/ethnic group's risk of a particular outcome to all other racial/ethnic groups. See Chapter 2 for more details.

Chapter 6

1. See Chapter 5 for more on the knowledge, skills, and abilities technical assistance providers need to support districts in addressing disproportionality.

2. For more information on CRPBIS, see http://crpbis.org/

3. The fourth ToT did not partake in supporting other ToTs.

4. The state attorney general found that Black students were three times more likely to be suspended than their white peers. Students with disabilities were twice as likely to be suspended as students without disabilities, and three times as likely to receive multiple suspensions in the same school year.

Chapter 7

1. Ally vs. Co-Conspirator: What it means to be an Abolitionist Teacher. April 20, 2019, interview with Dr. Yolanda Sealey-Ruiz. Found at: https://www.c-span.org/video/?c4844082/user-clip-ally-vs-conspirator-means-abolitionist-teacher

2. The authors of this report use quotation marks around CRT to signify the fact that opposition groups have used "CRT" to encompass almost any equity-driven work and rarely have defined the framework as originally and currently intended.

Appendix

1. "School district leaders" or "leaders" refers to superintendents, central office district administrators and school building principals and identified teacher leaders.

References

Aguilar, E. (2016). *The art of coaching teams: Building resilient communities that transform schools.* Jossey-Bass.

American Civil Liberties Union. (2020). *Police in schools continue to target Black, Brown, and Indigenous students with disabilities. The Trump Administration has data that's likely to prove it.* https://www.aclu.org/news/criminal-law-reform /police-in-schools-continue-to-target-black-brown-and-indigenous-students -with-disabilities-the-trump-administration-has-data-thats-likely-to-prove-it/

Annamma, S. A. (2018). *The pedagogy of pathologization.* Routledge.

Annamma, S. A., Jackson, D. D., & Morrison, D. (2016). Conceptualizing color-evasiveness: Using dis/ability critical race theory to expand a color-blind racial ideology in education and society. *Race Ethnicity and Education, 20*(2), 147–162. https://doi.org/10.1080/13613324.2016.1248837

Beale Spencer, M. (2006). Phenomenology and ecological systems theory: Development of divers groups. In R. M. Lerner & W. Damon (Eds.), *Handbook of child psychology: Theoretical models of human development* (pp. 829–893). John Wiley & Sons Inc.

Blasé, K. (2009). *Technical assistance to promote service and systemic change: Roadmap to intervention practices #4.* University of South Florida, Technical Assistance Center on Social Emotional Intervention for Young Children.

Bogotch, I. E. (2002). Educational leadership and social justice: Practice into theory. *Journal of School Leadership, 12*(2), 138–156.

Bonilla-Silva, E. (2003). *Racism without racists: Color-blind racism and the persistence of racial inequality in the United States.* Rowman & Littlefield.

Bryk, A. S., Bender Sebring, P., Allensworth, E., Luppescu, S., & Easton, J. Q. (2010). *Organizing for school improvement: Lessons from Chicago.* University of Chicago Press.

Carter, P. L., Skiba, R., Arrendondo, M. I., & Pollack, M. (2016). You can't fix what you don't look at: Acknowledging race in addressing racial disparities. *Urban Education, 52*(2), 207–235.

Clewell, B. C., Puma, M. J., & McKay, S. A. (2005). *Does it matter if my teacher looks like me? The impact of teacher race and ethnicity on student academic achievement.* Paper presented at Annual Meeting of the American Educational Research Association, Montreal, Canada.

Crenshaw, K. (1991). Mapping the margins: Intersectionality, identity politics, and violence against women of color. *Stanford Law Review, 43*(6), 1241–1299. https://doi.org/10.2307/1229039

Cross, W. E. (1995a). In search of blackness and Afrocentricity: The psychology of Black identity change. In H. W. Harris, H. C. Blue, & E. E. H. Griffith (Eds.), *Racial and ethnic identity* (pp. 53–72). Routledge.

Daud, Y., Yosuff, Z. J., Khalid, R., Don, Y., & Omar-Fauzee, M. S. (2015). Distributive leadership among leaders in effective schools. *Journal of Teaching and Education, 4*(3), 423–433.

Dee, T. E. (2004). The race connection: Are teachers more effective with students who share their own ethnicity? *Education Next, 4*(2), 1–8.

Dee, T. E. (2005). A teacher like me: Does race, ethnicity or gender matter? *American Economic Review, 95*(2), 158–165.

DiAngelo, R. (2018). *White fragility: Why it's so hard for white people to talk about racism?* Beacon Press.

Dobbin, F., & Kalev, A. (2018). Why doesn't diversity training work? The Challenge for industry and academia. *Anthropology Now, 10*(2), 48–55. DOI: 10.1080/19428200.2018.1493182

Easton-Brooks, D., Lewis, C., & Zhang, Y. (2009). Ethnic-matching: The influence of African American teachers on the reading scores of African American students. *The National Journal of Urban Education and Practice, 3*(1), 230–243.

Eddy, C., & Easton-Brooks, D. (2011). Ethnic matching, school placement, and mathematics achievement of African American students from kindergarten through fifth grade. *Urban Education, 46*(6), 1280–1299.

Elmore, R. (2004). *School reform from the inside out: Policy, practice, and performance.* Harvard University Press.

Fergus, E. (2017). *Solving disproportionality and achieving equity: A leader's guide to using data to change hearts and minds.* SAGE Publications.

Fergus, E. (2017). Confronting colorblindness. *Phi Delta Kappan, 98*(5), 30–35. https://doi.org/10.1177/0031721717690362

Fergus, E. (2019). Confronting our beliefs about poverty and discipline. *Phi Delta Kappan, 100*(5), 31–34. https://doi.org/10.1177/0031721719827542

Fraser, N. (2008). *Scales of justice: Reimagining political space in a globalizing world.* Polity.

Fread Albrecht, S., Skiba, R. J., Losen, D. J., Chung, C-G., & Middelberg, L. (2012). Federal policy on disproportionality in special education: Is it moving us forward? *Journal of Disability Policy Studies, 23*(1), 14–25.

Fullan, M., Rincon-Gallardo, S., & Hargreaves, A. (2015). Professional capital as accountability. *Education Policy Analysis Archives, 23*(15), 1–17. http://dx.doi.org/10.14507/epaa.v23.1998

Fullan, M., & Quinn, J. (2016). *Coherence: The right drivers in action for schools, districts, and Systems.* SAGE Publications.

Gay, G. (2000). *Culturally responsive teaching: Theory, research, and practice.* Teachers College Press.

Gilliam, W. S., Maupin, A. N., Reyes, C. R., Accavitti, M., & Shic, F. (2016). *Do early educators' implicit biases regarding sex and race relate to behavior expectations and recommendations of preschool expulsions and suspensions?* Child Study Center, Yale University.

González, T., & Artiles, A. J. (2020). Wrestling with the paradoxes of equity: A cultural-historical reframing of technical assistance interventions. *Multiple Voices, 20*(1), 5–15.

Gooden, M. A., & Dantley, M. (2012). Centering race in a framework for leadership preparation. *Journal of Research on Leadership Education, 7*(2), 237–253.

Gorski, P. (2019). Avoiding racial equity detours. *Educational Leadership, 76*(7), 56–61.

Great Lakes Equity Center. (2013). *Equity definition.* https://greatlakesequity.org/sites/default/files/201929041834_equity_digest.pdf

Gruenert, S., & Whitakter, T. (2015). *School culture rewired: How to define, assess, and transform it.* ASCD.

Guskey, T. R. (1985). Staff Development and teacher change. *Educational Leadership, 42*(7), 57–60.

Hambrick Hitt, D., Robinson, W., & Player, D. (2018). *District readiness to support school turnaround: A guide for state education agencies and districts* (2nd ed.). WestEd.

Hannay, L., Ben Jaafar, S., & Earl, L. (2013). A case study of district leadership using knowledge management for educational change. *Journal of Organizational Change Management, 26*(1), 64–82.

Harry, B., & Klingner, J. K. (2014). *Why are so many minority students in special education?: Understanding Race & Disability in Schools* (2nd ed.). Teachers College Press.

Helms, J. E. (1995). An update of Helms's White and people of color racial identity models. In J. G. Ponterotto, J. M. Casas, L. A. Suzuki, & C. M. Alexander (Eds.), *Handbook of multicultural counseling.* SAGE Publications.

Hester, P. P., Kaiser, A. P., Alpert, C. L., & Whiteman, B. (1995). The generalized effects of training trainers to teach parents to implement milieu teaching. *Journal of Early Intervention, 20*, 30–51.

Jackson, K. R., Fixsen, D., & Ward, C. (2018). Four domains for rapid school improvement: An implementation framework. *State implementation and scaling up of evidence based practices at the National Implementation Research Network, University of North Carolina at Chapel Hill.* https://files.eric.ed.gov/fulltext/ED606092.pdf

Jones, F. H., Fremouw, W., & Carples, S. (1977). Pyramid training of elementary school teachers to use a classroom management "skill package." *Journal of Applied Behavior Analysis, 10*, 239–253.

Khalifa, M. (2018). *Culturally responsive school leadership.* Harvard Education Press.

Khalifa, M., Gooden, M. A., & Davis, J. E. (2016). Culturally responsive school leadership: A synthesis of the literature. *Review of Educational Research, 86*(4), 1272–1311.

King-Sears, M. E., Walker, J. D., & Barry, C. (2018). Measuring teachers' intervention fidelity. *Intervention in School and Clinic, 54*(2), 89–96. https://doi.org/10.1177/1053451218765229

Klingner, J. K., Artiles, A. J., Kozleski, E., Harry, B., Zion, S., Tate, W., . . . & Riley, D. (2005). Addressing the disproportionate representation of culturally and linguistically diverse students in special education through culturally responsive educational systems. *Education Policy Analysis Archives, 13*(38), 2–40.

Knipp, H., & Stevenson, R. (2022). "A powerful visual statement": Race, class, and gender in uniform and dress code policies in New Orleans Public Charter Schools. *Affilia, 37*(1), 79–96. https://doi.org/10.1177/08861099211010026

Knowles, M. S. (1984). *Andragogy in action. Applying modern principles of adult education.* Jossey Bass.

Kramarczuk Voulgarides, C. (2018). *Does compliance matter in special education?: IDEA and the hidden inequities of practice.* Teachers College Press.

Kramarczuk Voulgarides, C., Aylward, A., Tefera, A., Artiles, A. J., Alvarado, S. L., & Noguera, P. (2021). Unpacking the logic of compliance in special education: Contextual influences on discipline racial disparities in suburban schools. *Sociology of Education, 94*(3), 208–226. http://doi.org/10.1177/00380407211013322

Kramarczuk Voulgarides, C., Fergus, E., & King Thorius, K. A. (2017). Pursuing equity: Disproportionality in special education and the reframing of technical solutions to address systemic inequities. *Review of Research in Education, 41*(1), 61–87. https://doi.org/10.3102/0091732X16686947

Kozleski, E. B., & Artiles, A. J. (2012). Technical assistance as inquiry: Using activity theory methods to engage equity in educational practice communities. In G. Canella & S. Steinberg (Eds.), *Critical Qualitative Research Reader* (pp. 408–419). Peter Lang.

Kuh, G. D., & Hutchings, P. (2015). Assessment and initiative fatigue: Keeping the focus on learning. *Using evidence of student learning to improve higher education* (pp. 183–200). Jossey-Bass.

Kumashiro, K. K. (2000). Toward a theory of anti-oppressive education. *Review of Educational Research, 70*(1), 25–53.

Lachat, M. A., & Smith, S. (2005). Practices that support data use in urban schools. *Journal of Education for Students Placed at Risk, 10*(3), 333–349.

Ladson-Billings, G. (1994). *The dreamkeepers: Successful teachers for African-American children.* Jossey-Bass.

Ladson-Billings, G. (1995a). But that's just good teaching! The case for culturally relevant pedagogy. *Theory into Practice, 34*(3), 159–165.

Ladson-Billings, G. (1995b). Toward a theory of culturally relevant pedagogy. *American Educational Research Journal, 32*(3), 465–491. https://doi.org/10.2307/1163320.

Ladson-Billings, G. (1998). Just what is critical race theory and what's it doing in a nice field like education? *Qualitative Studies in Education, 11*(1), 7–24.

Ladson-Billings, G. (2021). *Culturally relevant pedagogy asking a different question.* Teachers College Press.

Ladson-Billings, G., & Tate, W. F. (1995). Toward a critical race theory of education. *Teachers College Record, 97*, 47–68.

Lave, J., & Wenger, E. (1991). *Learning in doing: Social, cognitive, and computational perspectives.* Cambridge University Press.

Learning for Justice. (2018). White privilege definition. https://www.learningforjustice.org/magazine/fall-2018/what-is-white-privilege-really

Lee, E., Menkart, D., & Okazawa-Rey, M. (2002). *Beyond heroes and holidays: A practical guide to K 12 anti-racist, multicultural education and staff development.* Teaching for change.

Leithwood, K. (1994). Leadership for school restructuring. *Educational Administration Quarterly, 30*(4), 498–518.

Leithwood, K., Harris, A., & Hopkins, D. (2020). Seven strong claims about successful school leadership revisited. *School Leadership and Management, 40*(1), 5–22.

Leithwood, K., & Jantzi, D. (1990). Transformational leadership: How principals can help reform school cultures. *School Effectiveness and Improvement, 1*(4), 249–280.

Lorde, A. (1997). The uses of anger. *Women's Studies Quarterly, 25*(1/2), 278–285.

Losen, D.J., Hodson, C.L., E, J., & Martinez, T.E. (2013). Disturbing inequities: Exploring the relationship between racial disparities in special education identification and discipline. *The Journal of Applied Research on Children: Informing Policy for Children at Risk, 5*(15), 1–20.

Love, B. L. (2019). *We want to do more than survive: Abolitionist teaching and the pursuit of educational freedom.* Beacon Press.

Malone, H.S, Rizkalla, D., & Bartlett, E. (2020). *Interrogating, interrupting and eradicating disproportionality through youth voice and actions: A guide for youth-adult partnership in pursuit of educational equity.* The Metropolitan Center for Research on Equity and the Transformation of Schools. https://steinhardt.nyu .edu/metrocenter/iesc/interrogating-interrupting-and-eradicating-disproportionality -through-youth-voice

Mehta, J. (2020, November 11). *Equity work: Too much talk, too little action.* Next generation learning challenges. https://www.nextgenlearning.org/articles /equity-work-too-much-talk-too-little-action

Meiners, E. R. (2007). *Right to be hostile: Schools, prisons, and the making of public enemies.* Taylor & Francis Group.

Milner, R. H. (2013). Rethinking achievement gap talk in urban education. *Urban Education, 48*(1), 3–8.

Milner, R. H. (2020). *Start where you are, but don't stay there: Understanding diversity, opportunity gaps, and teaching in today's classrooms* (2nd ed.). Harvard Education Press.

Mulford, B., & Silins, H. (2003). Leadership for organisational learning and improved student outcomes—What do we know? *Cambridge Journal of Education, 33*(2), 175–195.

Neville, H. A., Lilly, R. L, Duran, G., Lee, R. M., & Browne, L. (2000). Construction and initial validation of the Color-Blind Racial Attitudes Scale (CoBRAS). *Journal of Counseling Psychology, 47,* 59–70.

New York State Education Department. (2013). *NYSED State Performance Plan (SPP) for 2005–2012—Revised February 2013—Indicator 4 overview of the state performance plan development.* https://www.p12.nysed.gov/specialed/spp /2013/ind4.htm

New York State Education Department. (2019). *Culturally Responsive-Sustaining Education Framework.* https://www.nysed.gov/crs/framework

Orfaly, R. A., Frances, J. C., Campbell, P., Whittemore, B., Joly, B., & Koh, H. (2005). Train-the-trainer as an educational model in public health preparedness. *Journal of Public Health Management Practice, 11*(6), S123–S127.

Paris, D. (2012). Culturally sustaining pedagogy: A needed change in stance, terminology, and practice. *Educational Researcher, 41*(3), 93–97. https://doi .org/10.3102/0013189X12441244

Paris, D. (2017). *On culturally sustaining teachers. Equity by design: Midwest & Plains Equity Assistance Center (MAP EAC).* http://glec.education.iupui.edu /Images/Briefs/DParis_onculturallysustainingteachers.pdf

Park, V., & Datnow, A. (2009). Co-constructing distributed leadership: District and school connection in data-driven decision making. *School Leadership and Management, 29*(5), 477–494.

Parsons, M. B., & Reid, D. H. (1995). Training residential supervisors to provide feedback for maintaining staff teaching skills with people who have severe disabilities. *Journal of Applied Behavior Analysis, 28,* 317–322.

Pollock, M., Deckman, S., Mira, M., & Shalaby, C. (2010). "But What Can I Do?": Three necessary tensions in teaching teachers about race. *Journal of Teacher Education, 61*(3), 211–224. https://doi.org/10.1177/0022487109354089

Pollock, M., Rogers, J., Kwako, A., Matschiner, A., Kendall, R., Bingener, C., Reece, E., Kennedy, B., & Howard, J. (2022). *The Conflict Campaign: Exploring local experiences of the campaign to ban "Critical Race Theory" in public K–12 education in the U.S., 2020–2021.* UCLA's Institute for Democracy, Education, and Access.

Roderick, M. (2012). Drawing in data but thirsty for analysis. *Teachers College Record, 114,* 1–9.

Rushovich, B. R., Bartley, L. H., Steward, R. K., & Bright, C. L. (2015). Technical assistance: A comparison between providers and recipients. *Human Service Organizations: Management, Leadership & Governance, 39*(4), 362–379.

Shalaby, C. (2016). *Troublemakers: Lessons from children disrupting school.* The New Press.

Siegel-Hawley, G., Bridges, K., & Shields, T. J. (2016). Solidifying segregation or promoting diversity?: School closure and rezoning in an urban district. *Educational Administration Quarterly, 53*(1), 107–141.

Skiba, R. J. (2013). CCBD's position summary on federal policy on disproportionality in special education. *Behavior Disorders, 38*(2), 108–120.

Skiba, R. J., Artiles, A. J., Kozleski, E. B., Losen, D. J., & Harry, E. G. (2016). Risks and consequences of oversimplifying educational inequities: A response to Morgan et al. (2015). *Educational Researcher, 45*(3), 221–225. https://doi.org/10.3102/0013189X16644606

Skiba, R. J., Michael, R. S., Nardo, A. C., & Peterson R. L. (2002). The color of discipline: Sources of racial and gender disproportionality in school punishment. *The Urban Review, 34*(4), 317–342. https://doi.org/10.1023/A:1021320817372

Skiba, R. J., Simmons, A. B., Ritter, S., Gibbs, A. C., Rausch, M., Cuadrado, J., & Chung C-G. (2008). Achieving equity in special education: History, status and current challenges. *Exceptional Children, 74*(3), 264–288.

Skiba, R. J., & Williams, N. T. (2016). *Are the Black kids worse? Myths and facts about racial differences in behavior: A summary of the literature.* The Equity Project at Indiana University.

Speck, M. (1996). Best practice in professional development for sustained educational change. *ERS Spectrum, 14*(2), 33–41. https://doi.org/:10.4135/9781446247150.n15

Spencer, M. B., Harpalani, V., Cassidy, E., Jacobs, C. Y., Donde, S., Goss, T. N., Muñoz-Miller, M., Charles, N., & Wilson, S. (2006). Understanding vulnerability and resilience from a normative developmental perspective: Implications for racially and ethnically diverse youth. In D. Cicchetti, & D. J. Cohen (Eds.), *Developmental psychopathology: Theory and method* (pp. 627–672). John Wiley & Sons, Inc.

Steele, C. (2011). *Whistling Vivaldi: How stereotypes affect us and what we can do.* W.W. Norton and Company.

Sullivan, A. L., & Osher, D. (2019). IDEA's double bind: A synthesis of disproportionality policy interpretations. *Exceptional Children, 85*(4), 395–412. https://doi.org/10.1177/0014402918818047

Swanson, J., & Welton, A. (2018). When good intentions only go so far: White principals leading discussions about race. *Urban Education, 54*(5), 732–759. https://doi.org/10.1177/0042085918783825

Tatum, B. D. (2003). *"Why are all the Black kids sitting together in the cafeteria?": And other conversations about race.* Basic Books.

Theoharis, G. (2007). Social justice educational leaders and resistance: Toward a theory of social justice leadership. *Educational Administration Quarterly, 43*(2), 221–258.

Valencia, R. R. (1997). *The evolution of deficit thinking: Educational thought and practice.* Falmer Press.

Wald, M., & Losen, D. (2003). *Deconstructing the school to prison pipeline.* Jossey-Bass.

Warner, S., & Duncan, E. (2019). *A vision and guidance for a diverse and learner-ready teacher workforce.* Council of Chief State School Officers.

Index

About the Authors

Dr. María G. Hernández has over a decade of experience providing technical assistance, training, and consultancy to districts, schools, and educational institutions to address race, ethnicity, language, and ability disproportionate outcomes. She coaches K–12 educators in developing systems that address disproportionality and equity by providing technical assistance and training. She supports districts and schools in building their capacity in Culturally Responsive-Sustaining Education (CR-SE), creating equity visions, data-driven culture, instructional leadership, positive school climate, family and community engagement, and devising action plans with multiple districts in making changes to system policies and practices to develop equitable educational systems. Her approach of relying on evidence-based research, implementation science, culturally responsive equitable systems, and developing ongoing transformative relationships in educational institutions has led to shifting mindsets, policies, practices, and procedures. She holds an MSW and PhD in social welfare from the University of Wisconsin, Madison, and an MA in educational leadership from New York University.

At the time of publication, *David Lopez* is a senior technical assistance specialist with WestEd's Talent Development and Diversity team. Lopez delivers technical assistance (TA) and expert consultation, develops research-and evidence-based tools and resources, and provides research and policy support to state education agencies, district leaders, and school-based educators, focused on creating culturally responsive and equitable systems, and completes comprehensive Systemic Equity Reviews for LEAs and SEAs. Lopez is also an expert facilitator and trainer on issues related to racial equity, intersectionality (e.g., race and ability), diversity, disproportionality, and culturally responsive-sustaining education. Prior to joining WestEd, Lopez was a senior equity associate at New York University's Metropolitan Center for Research on Equity and the Transformation of Schools (Metro Center), providing training and technical assistance to educators to implement the statewide framework for Culturally Responsive-Sustaining Education and to create equitable systems.

Lopez received an MA in educational leadership, politics, and advocacy from New York University, Steinhardt, and a BA in political science from Haverford College.

Reed Swier is an associate director of training and development at The Metropolitan Center for Research on Equity and the Transformation of Schools at NYU Steinhardt, focused on promoting equity and opportunity in education. Currently, his work with NYU Metro's Innovations in Equity and Systemic Change (IESC) focuses on building capacity for educational institutions in understanding and responding to systems of inequality that disproportionately impact historically marginalized students and families.

Reed has taught for over a decade in elementary schools in Oakland, California, and New York City. As a school administrator, Reed supported staff, students, and families by promoting culturally responsive teaching and developing a school culture philosophy and practice embedded in restorative approaches. In 2018, Reed lived in Scotland as a Fulbright Scholar, participating in the Fulbright Distinguished Awards in Teaching program where he worked with local educators and University of Edinburgh students and faculty around issues of racial identity, whiteness, and restorative practices. Reed partnered with the Centre for Education for Racial Equality in Scotland (CERES) where he continues to be an associate.

Reed holds a BA from the University of Michigan, an MS in teaching grades 1–6 from Pace University, and an MEd in learning and teaching from the Harvard Graduate School of Education.